PIANO · VOCAL · GUITAR

Mary J. Blige
Reflections (A Retrospective)

MJB

W9-BXM-975

2 Reflections (I Remember)

12 We Ride (I See the Future)

20 You Know

28 King & Queen

34 No More Drama

44 Family Affair

52 Real Love

57 No One Will Do

64 Be Without You

71 I'm Going Down

75 911

82 Not Gon' Cry

87 My Life '06

97 Be Happy

104 I'll Be There for You/You're All I Need to Get By

ISBN 978-1-4234-2874-9

HAL•LEONARD® CORPORATION

7777 W. Bluemound Rd. P.O. Box 13819 Milwaukee, WI 53213

For all works contained herein:
Unauthorized copying, arranging, adapting,
recording or public performance is an infringement of copyright.
Infringers are liable under the law.

Visit Hal Leonard Online at
www.halleonard.com

REFLECTIONS
(I Remember)

Words and Music by MARY J. BLIGE, JOHNTA AUSTIN,
BRYAN MICHAEL COX and KENDRICK DEAN

Moderate Hip-Hop

* *Recorded a half step higher.*

Copyright © 2006 UNIVERSAL MUSIC CORP., MARY J. BLIGE MUSIC, CHRYSALIS MUSIC, NAKED UNDER MY CLOTHES, W.B.M. MUSIC CORP.,
DECEMBER FIRST PUBLISHING GROUP, INC., NOONTIME SOUTH INC., SONGS IN THE KEY OF B FLAT, INC. and THE DEAN'S LIST
All Rights for MARY J. BLIGE MUSIC Controlled and Administered by UNIVERSAL MUSIC CORP.
All Rights for NAKED UNDER MY CLOTHES Administered by CHRYSALIS MUSIC
All Rights Reserved Used by Permission

Gm
3fr
F
Cm9
Dm
- ber.
I re - mem - ber.
Gm
3fr
F
E♭maj7
F
Back be - fore the rec - ord deal and the cars and the cribs and the way that things took
Gm
3fr
F
Cm9
Dm
off, I was sing - in' at Lu - cy's on one - twen - ty - fifth just try - in' my best to get
Gm
3fr
F
E♭maj7
F
on. Back when me and Puff and B.I.G. was kids and I knew Jo - de -

Gm
3fr
F
Cm9
Dm
ci, I was young and tough and fresh and rough and it was all a
Gm
3fr
F
E♭maj7
F
dream. Sign - in' a con - tract. No guid - ing light but just hop - in' I,
Gm
3fr
F
Cm9
Dm
I can get out the proj - ects and get my fam - ily right 'cause they were my life.
Gm
3fr
F
E♭maj7
F
In a red zone and a Bent - ley's you can catch me tryin' to do

Gm
3fr
F
Cm9
Dm
me. I was jad - ed on the block. I could - a fad - ed on the block but I made it off the block and I,
Gm
3fr
F
E♭maj7
F
(I re - mem - ber) back when I did - n't know which way to feel.
Gm
3fr
F
Cm9
Dm
(I re - mem - ber) back when pain was all I had to give.
Gm
3fr
F
E♭maj7
F
(The re - flec - tions of my life I see, the les - sons that I've learned,

Gm
3fr
F
Cm9
Dm
To Coda
and now I know)
heart - break don't ex - ist when it's been torn

Gm
3fr
F
E♭maj7
F
a - part by love. I used to throw a fit. I used to shut it down and blame it on a

Gm
3fr
F
Cm9
Dm
man.
But that was Mar - y then and this is Mar - y now, you got - ta un - der -

Gm
3fr
F
E♭maj7
F
stand. It's a - bout how we re - spect our - selves and the men have no con - trol

Gm
3fr
F
Cm9
Dm
of our self - es - teem, and when we see that then we can let

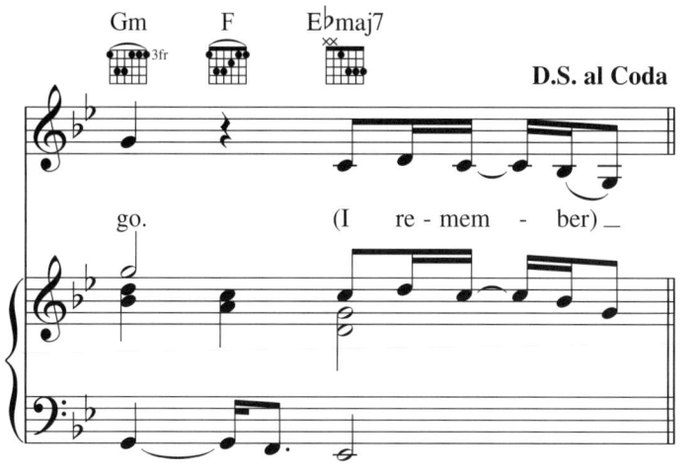
Gm
3fr
F
E♭maj7
D.S. al Coda
go. (I re - mem - ber)

CODA
N.C.
a - part by love. Now, I

made some mis - takes. I lost some friends a - long the way, but I

Dm
Gm
3fr
F
E♭maj7
don't car - ry it be - cause it's made me a bet - ter chick. It's my life and

F
Gm
3fr
F
Cm9
I know that there's more for me to see. I may not be what I'm sup-posed to
Dm
Gm
3fr
F
E♭maj7
but I can tell you right now I ain't what I used to be.
(I re-mem - ber.)
F
Gm
3fr
F
Cm9
I re-mem-ber when I did-n't know which way to feel.
(I re-mem - ber.) I re-
Dm
Gm
3fr
F
E♭maj7
mem-ber when pain was all I had to give.
The re-flec - tions of my life

F
Gm
3fr
F
Cm9
I see, the les - sons that I've learned, and now I know
Dm
Gm
3fr
F
E♭maj7
heart - break don't ex - ist when it's been torn a - part by love.
(I re - mem - ber.)
F
Gm
3fr
F
Cm9
I re - mem - ber, I re - mem - ber when.
(I re - mem - ber.)
Dm
Gm
3fr
F
E♭maj7
I re - mem - ber, I re - mem - ber.
The re - flec - tions of my life

F
Gm
3fr
F
Cm9
I see, the les - sons that I've learned, and now I know
Dm
Gm
3fr
F
E♭maj7
heart - break don't ex - ist when it's been torn a - part by love.
(I re - mem - ber.)
F
Gm
3fr
F
Cm9
(Lead vocal ad lib.)
(I re - mem - ber.)
Dm
Gm
3fr
F
E♭maj7
(I re - mem - ber.)

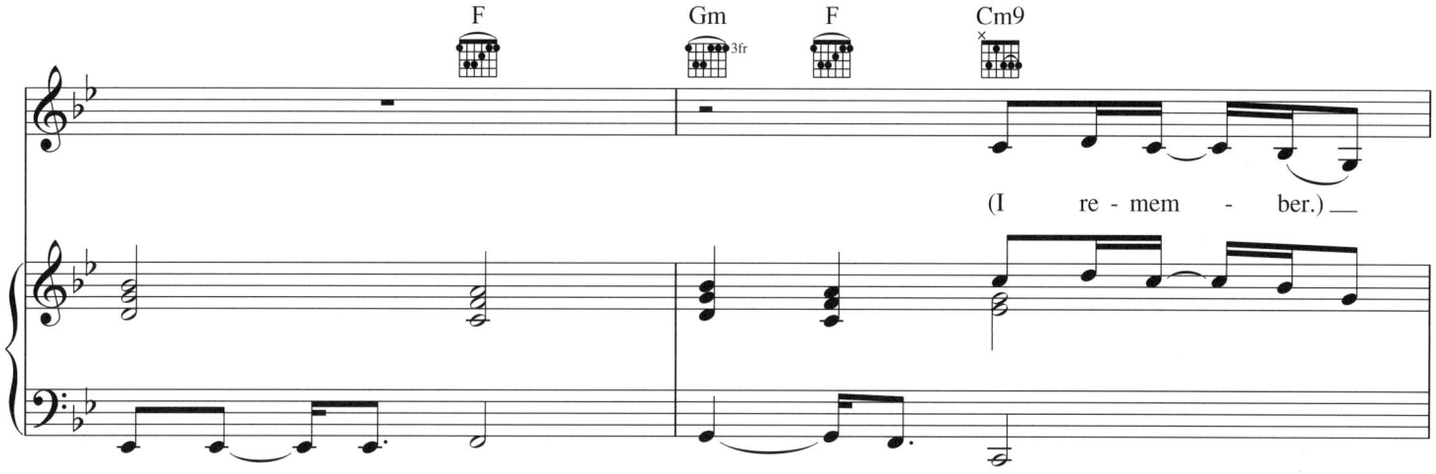
F
Gm
3fr
F
Cm9
(I re - mem - ber.)

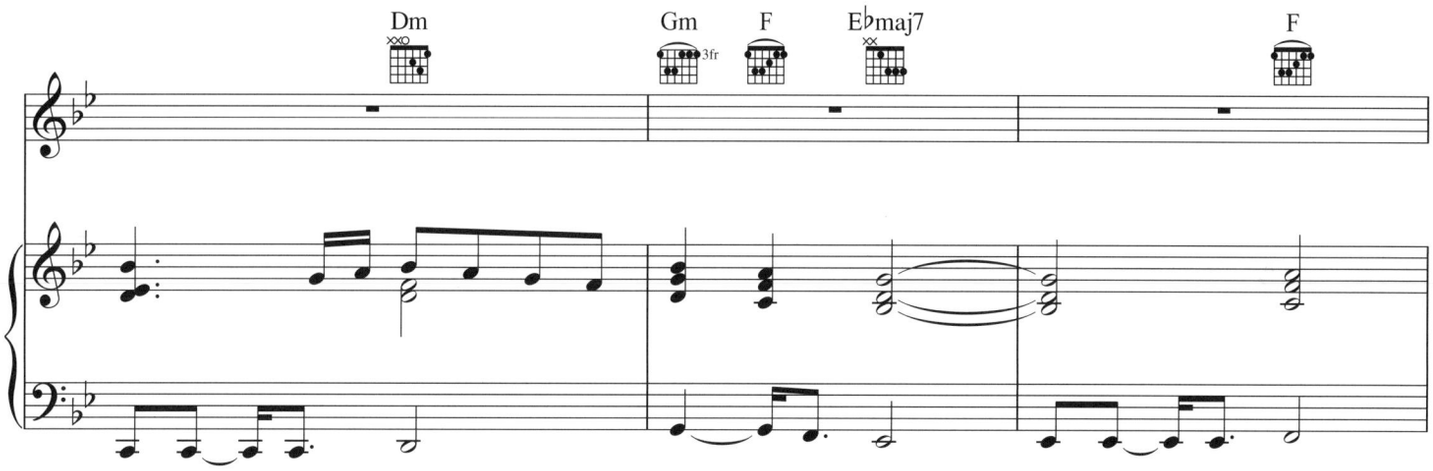
Dm
Gm
3fr
F
E♭maj7
F

Gm
3fr
F
Cm9
Dm
Gm
3fr
F
E♭maj7

F
Gm
3fr
F
Cm9
Dm
(I re - mem - ber.)

WE RIDE
(I See the Future)

Words and Music by MARY J. BLIGE, JOHNTA AUSTIN,
BRYAN MICHAEL COX and KENDRICK DEAN

* *Recorded a half step lower.*

Copyright © 2006 UNIVERSAL MUSIC CORP., MARY J. BLIGE MUSIC, CHRYSALIS MUSIC, NAKED UNDER MY CLOTHES, W.B.M. MUSIC CORP.,
DECEMBER FIRST PUBLISHING GROUP, INC., NOONTIME SOUTH INC., SONGS IN THE KEY OF B FLAT, INC. and THE DEAN'S LIST
All Rights for MARY J. BLIGE MUSIC Controlled and Administered by UNIVERSAL MUSIC CORP.
All Rights for NAKED UNDER MY CLOTHES Administered by CHRYSALIS MUSIC
All Rights Reserved Used by Permission

N.C.
Ev -'ry - bod - y ask - in' why Mar - y ain't mad no more, (no more, no more, no more.) It
seems like a ques - tion that I've al - read - y an - swered like too man - y times be - fore. Now, la - dies,
Bm
Gmaj7
F♯m
D
Em
F♯sus
F♯
if you got a man and he treats you real good, ain't you gon' flex ev -'ry chance that you get now?
G
Dmaj9
C♯m11
F♯sus
F♯
Ain't you gon' love him just like you should, 'spe - cially when you nev - er thought you would, yeah?

Bm Gmaj7 F♯m D Em F♯sus F♯
Oh, you know that I'm all in - to the feel - in' and I nev - er look to lose it.
G Dmaj9 C♯m11 F♯sus F♯
Oh, for sure this is con - sis - tent. With you I find a rhy - thm. From the
𝄋
Bm Gmaj7 F♯m D Em F♯sus F♯
day to the night we ride, we ride, we ride. Hey, now how you like it, how you like it now?
G Dmaj9 C♯m11 F♯sus F♯
I see the fu - ture, ba - by. You and I, bet - ter with time. And it is

Bm Gmaj7 F♯m D Em F♯sus F♯
what it is and I just can't help it.
And I felt what I felt. No, I just can't help it.
To Coda
G Dmaj9 C♯m11 F♯sus F♯
I see the fu - ture, ba - by. Me and you, that's how we do. I got a
Bm Gmaj7 F♯m D Em F♯sus F♯
song in my heart, it's all that I need. I sing it a cap - pel - la. I sing it to the beat.
G Dmaj9 C♯m11 F♯sus F♯
What we are is clas - sic, you know it be-cause your at - ti - tude shows it. Now, fel - las,

Bm
Gmaj7
F♯m
D
Em
F♯sus
F♯
if you got a girl and she treats you right, ain't you gon' spend ev-'ry dol-lar, ev-'ry cent, hey?
G
Dmaj9
C♯m11
F♯sus
F♯
D.S. al Coda
Ain't you gon' make sure she stay fly, 'spe-cially when she rep-pin' you for life? From the
CODA
C♯m11
F♯sus
F♯
Bm
N.C.
Me and you, that's how we do. You are mine, I told you be-fore. I would-n't
G
D
lie, I need you and more. Got-ta stay with you.

C♯m7♭5
F♯7
N.C.
I am safe with you. Let me re - peat it in case you for - got. Love is a
Gmaj7
D
moun - tain and we're at the top, yeah. Breath and strength all the time,
C♯m7♭5
F♯7
Bm
Gmaj7
F♯m
D
see the fu - ture in your eye.
From the day to the night, we ride, we ride, we
(Lead vocal ad lib.)
Em
F♯sus
F♯
G
Dmaj9
ride.
I see the fu - ture, ba - by.

C♯m11 F♯sus F♯ Bm Gmaj7 F♯m D
You and I, bet - ter with time. And it is what it is. And I felt
Em F♯sus F♯ G Dmaj9 C♯m11 F♯sus F♯
what I felt. I see the fu - ture, ba - by. Me and you, that's how we do. From the
Bm Gmaj7 F♯m D Em F♯sus F♯
day to the night, we ride, we ride, we ride.
G Dmaj9 C♯m11 F♯sus F♯
I see the fu - ture, ba - by. You and I, bet - ter with time. And it is

Bm
Gmaj7
F♯m
D
Em
F♯sus
F♯
what it is.
And I felt what I felt.
G
Dmaj9
C♯m11
F♯sus
F♯
I see the fu - ture, ba - by.
Me and you, that's how we do.
Bm
Gmaj7
F♯m
D
Em
F♯sus
F♯
Ooh,
Repeat and Fade
Opt. Ending
G
Dmaj9
C♯m11
F♯sus
F♯
Bm
just can't help it, I love my hun.
All that I need and all that I want. Said,

YOU KNOW

Words and Music by MARY J. BLIGE,
SEAN GARRETT and ERIC HUDSON

Copyright © 2006 UNIVERSAL MUSIC CORP., MARY J. BLIGE MUSIC, HITCO MUSIC, TEAM S DOT PUBLISHING,
WARNER-TAMERLANE PUBLISHING CORP. and E. HUDSON MUSIC, LLC
All Rights for MARY J. BLIGE MUSIC Controlled and Administered by UNIVERSAL MUSIC CORP.
All Rights for HITCO MUSIC and TEAM S DOT PUBLISHING Administered by SONGS OF WINDSWEPT PACIFIC
All Rights for E. HUDSON MUSIC, LLC Administered by WARNER-TAMERLANE PUBLISHING CORP.
All Rights Reserved Used by Permission

know, when you know, know, know, know, _ know, know, know right. Know when you know, you know, _ you know, know right. You

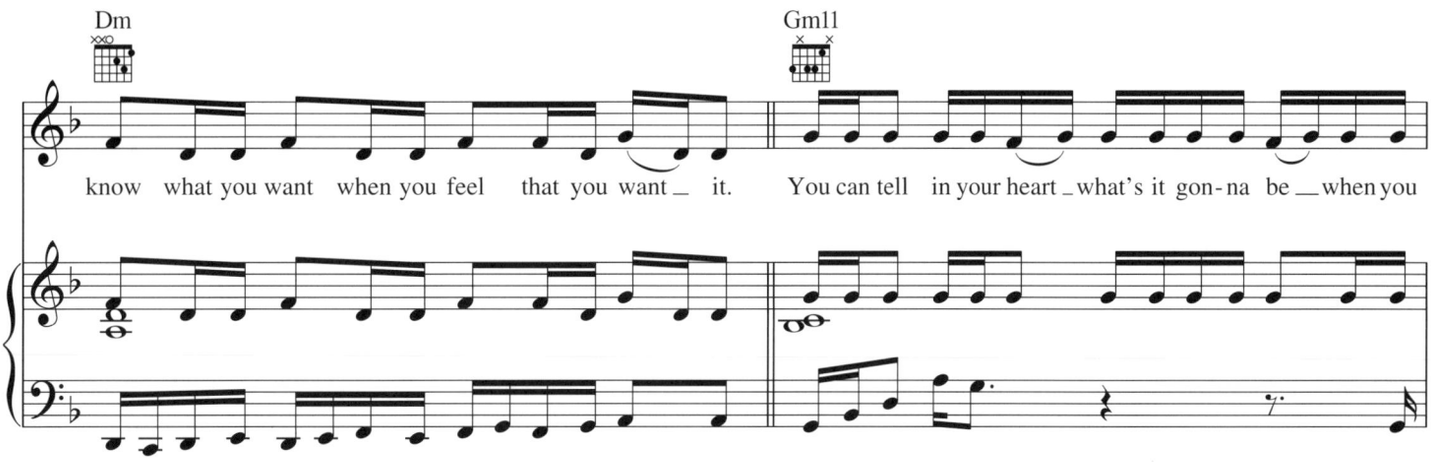
Dm
Gm11
know what you want when you feel that you want _ it.
You can tell in your heart _ what's it gon-na be _ when you

feel the fire _____ like when you're hold - in' me. ___
I took a chance _ on your song and dance, _ made me feel like

Dm7
Gm11
plans _ could be made for us both to be _____ lov-ers and friends _'til the end, _ when it's not a sin. _
(D.S.) Lov-ers and friends _'til the end, _ when it's not a sin. _

Nev - er would - 've thought it was you that would choose me.

Now I'm on the flight, ain't a - fraid of heights. I can breathe

Dm7
Gm7
C
fine, ex - hale 'cause you did some - thin' to me.
When you made me feel love, real - ly made me give up when I

Gm7
C
did - n't see much, when I felt your touch. What a man say once in the first twelve months, I ain't

Gm7
Dm7
heard all my life from the clos - est one.
There's so much I knew, too good to be true when it
Gm7
came so fast. What's a girl to do? Nev - er will I say, when a man won't change, that you
Dm9
3fr
N.C.
changed my life and I'm so damn hap - py, babe. Know when you know, you know, you know, know when you
know, when you know, know, know, know, know, know, know right. Know when you know, you know, you know, know right. You

know what you want when you feel that you want _ it. Know when you know, you know, _ you know, know when you

To Coda
know, when you know, know, know, know, _ know, know, know right. Know when you know, you know, _ you know, know right. You

Gm11
know what you want when you feel that you want _ it.
Ev-'ry time a knock _ was a knock, _ give'em e-qual time _ so I

know _ that it's me, _ that it's me _ that you're look-in' for. Lit-tle hug, _ then a kiss, _ just show me you miss _ me and

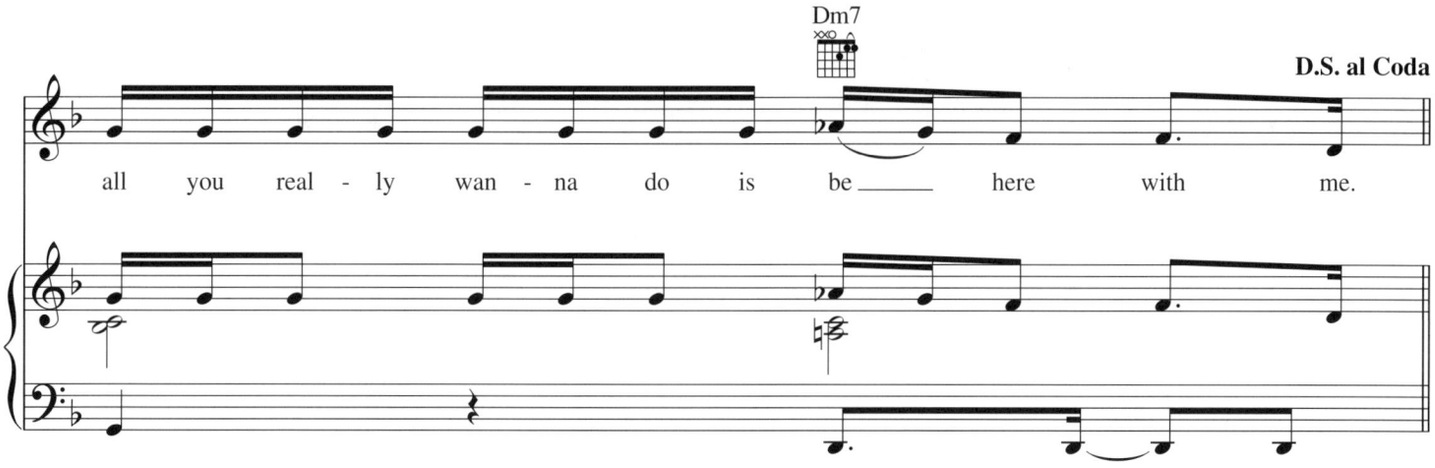
Dm7
D.S. al Coda
all you real - ly wan - na do is be here with me.

CODA
Dbmaj7
know what you want when you feel that you want it.
You know

Fmaj7
Dbmaj7
when you real - ly know.
You know in your heart

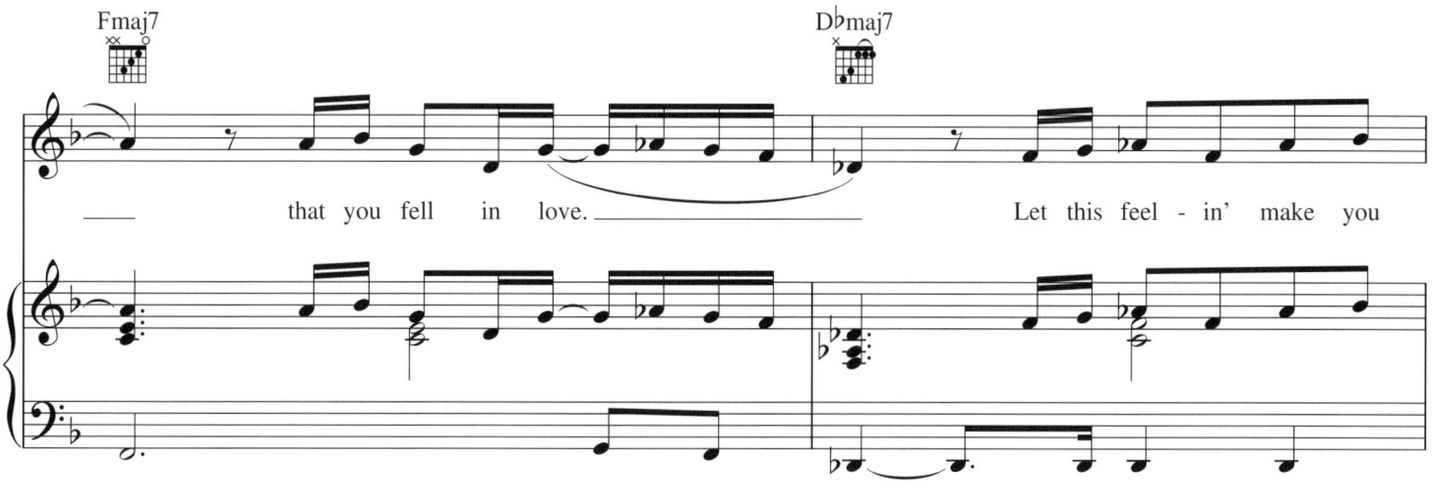
Fmaj7
Dbmaj7
that you fell in love.
Let this feel - in' make you

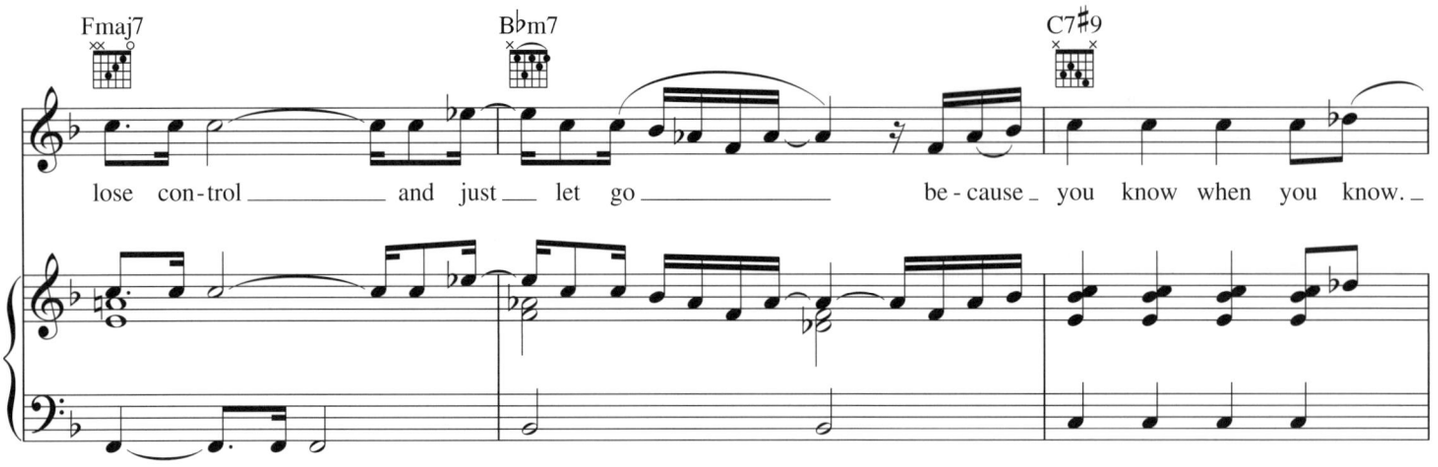
Fmaj7
B♭m7
C7♯9
lose con-trol and just let go be-cause you know when you know.

N.C.
You know. You

know what you want when you feel that you want it. Know when you know, you know, you know, know when you

know,when you know,know,know, know, know,know, know right. Know when you know, you know, you know, know right.You

Gm11
Play 3 times
know what you want when you feel that you want it.

Dm7
8va

Gm11
You
8va

Dm7
N.C.
know what you want when you feel that you want it.
Want it, want it, want it, want it.

KING & QUEEN

Words and Music by STEVIE WONDER,
JOHN STEPHENS and AVRIELE CRANDLE

© 2006 JOBETE MUSIC CO., INC., BLACK BULL MUSIC, CHERRY RIVER MUSIC CO., JOHN LEGEND PUBLISHING, SONGS OF KOBALT MUSIC PUBLISHING and LIL RED ROOM PUBLISHING
JOBETE MUSIC CO., INC. and BLACK BULL MUSIC
c/o EMI APRIL MUSIC INC.
Worldwide Rights for JOHN LEGEND PUBLISHING Administered by CHERRY RIVER MUSIC CO.
All Rights Reserved International Copyright Secured Used by Permission
- contains a sample of "Visions" by Stevie Wonder

E♭m9
4fr
back when I met you at school
I looked in your eyes, saw some-thing spe-cial in you.
Fm9
E♭m9
4fr
We as - pi - re that we live the A - mer - i - can dream.
Es - cape this re - al - i - ty,
Fm9
come start a new one with me.
We could be neigh - bor - hood roy - al - ty or much
3
3
3
3
E♭m9
4fr
Fm9
more than that, you see. We're mak - in' his - to - ry. We'll go to the max,

E♭m9
4fr
fly to heav-en and back. The high-est heights we'll match. Yes, we can do all of that, ba-by.

Fm9
E♭m9
4fr
La, la, la, la, la, la, la, la, la, la, la, we could be king and queen some-

Fm9
day. La, la, la, la, la, la, la, la, la, la, la, we'll nev-er

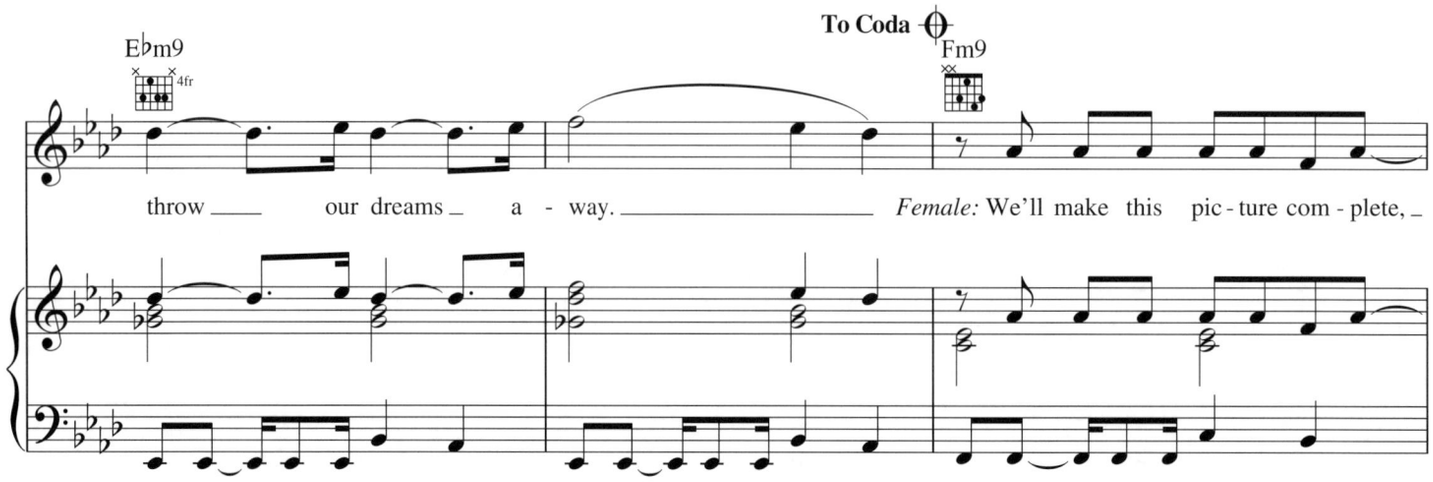
E♭m9
4fr
To Coda
Fm9
throw our dreams a-way.
Female: We'll make this pic-ture com-plete,

E♭m9
4fr
start a new fam - i - ly. A boy that looks just like you, a girl that looks just like me.
Fm9
E♭m9
4fr
And each day that they grow, we'll teach them all that we know. Help me show them the way.
Fm9
3
We'll show them we're not a - fraid to be free, the on - ly thing that should be. The
E♭m9
4fr
Fm9
3
fly - est fan - ta - sies, the high - est they can dream. Grab hold to my hand,

E♭m9
say that you'll be my man. Some-day you'll be my king and, ba-by, I'm your queen to be.
Fm9
D.S. al Coda
Male:
La, la, la, la, la, la, la, la,
CODA
D♭m7
G♭
Male: Cit - ies may crum - ble, the
E♭m7
A♭6
D♭m7
G♭
E♭m7
A♭6
world is in trou - ble, but we'll be in love and we'll rise a - bove it.
D♭m7
G♭
E♭m7
A♭6
D♭m7
G♭
Each of our peo - ple pray for a lead - er. I know we could be some-day,

E♭m7
6fr
Em7
Fm9
E♭m9
4fr
some - day,
some - day,

Fm9
some - day.
La, la, la, la, la, la, la, la, la, la, la,
we'll nev - er

E♭m9
4fr
Fm9
throw our dreams a - way.
La, la, la, la, la, la, la, la, la, la, la,
we could be

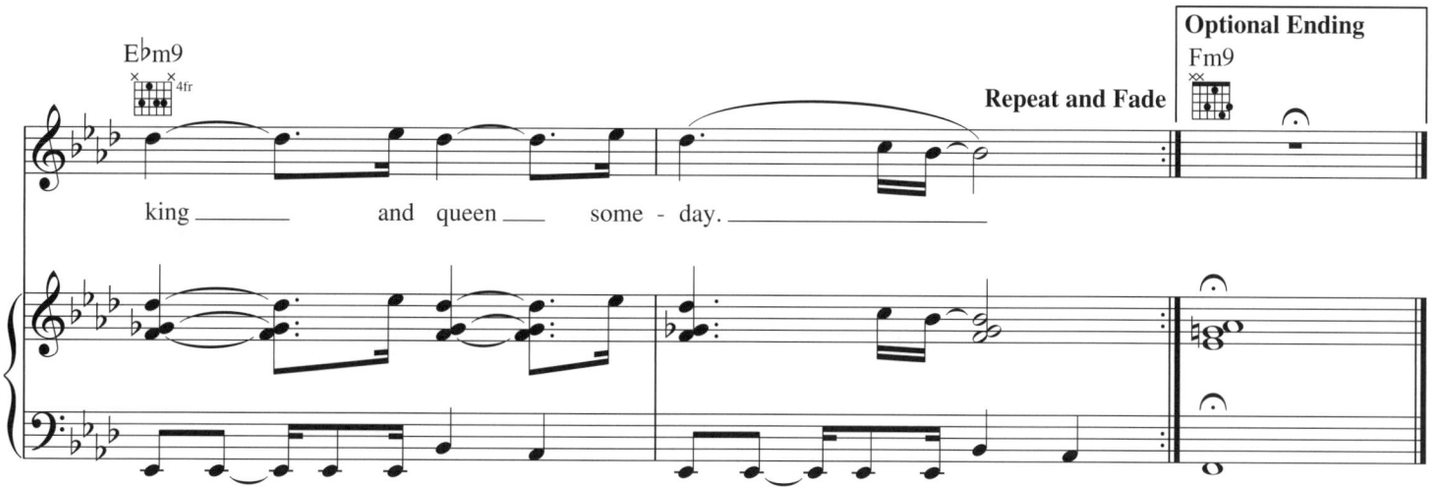
E♭m9
4fr
king and queen some - day.
Repeat and Fade
Optional Ending
Fm9

NO MORE DRAMA

Words and Music by JAMES HARRIS III, TERRY LEWIS,
BARRY DeVORZON and PERRY BOTKIN

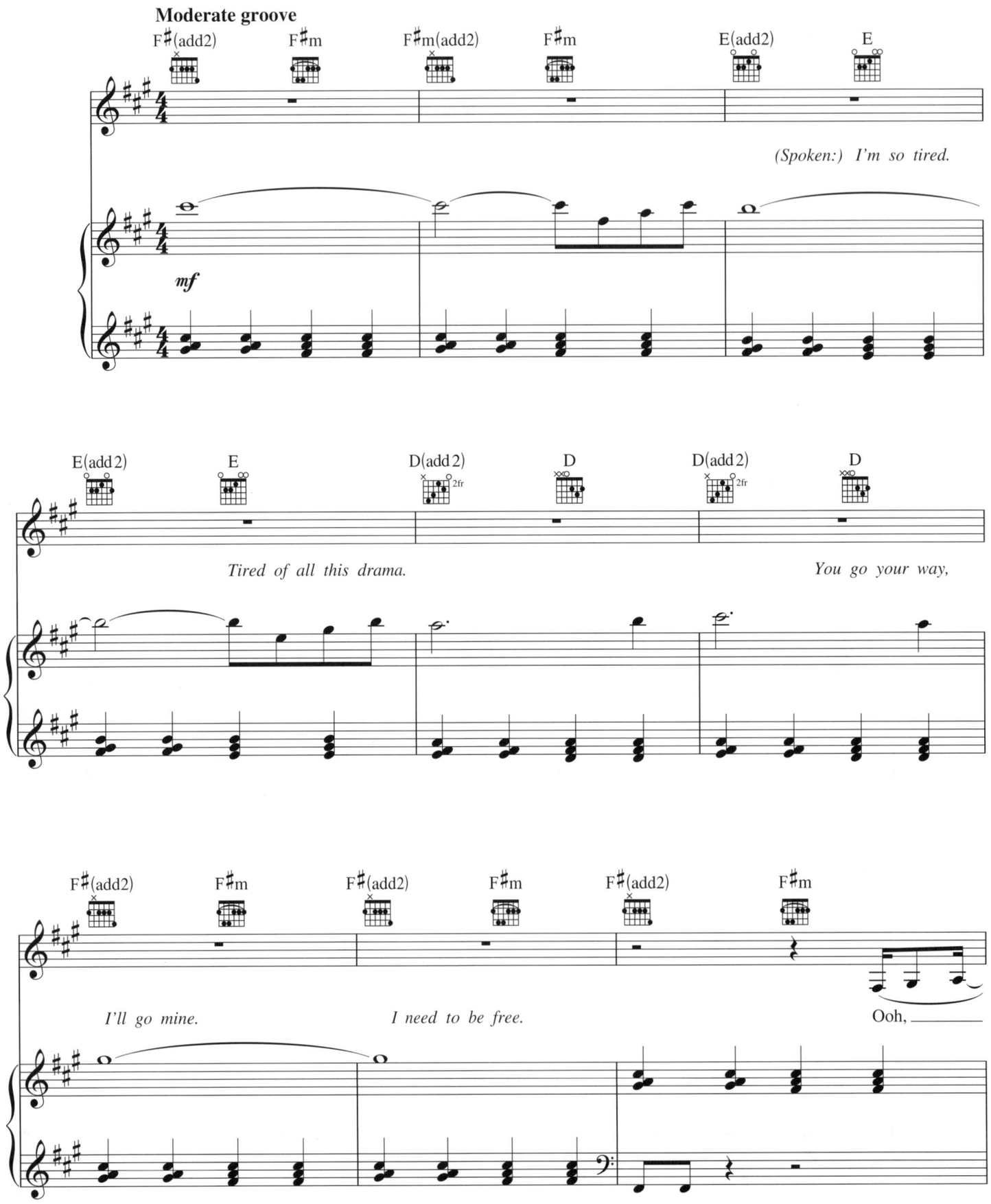

© 2001 EMI APRIL MUSIC INC., FLYTE TYME TUNES INC. and SCREEN GEMS-EMI MUSIC INC.
All Rights for FLYTE TYME TUNES INC. Controlled and Administered by EMI APRIL MUSIC INC.
All Rights Reserved International Copyright Secured Used by Permission
- contains elements of "The Young and the Restless"

F♯(add2)
F♯m
E(add2)
E
E(add2)
E
ooh, no more, no more. Umm,
I'm so tired, tired, tired of all this drama.

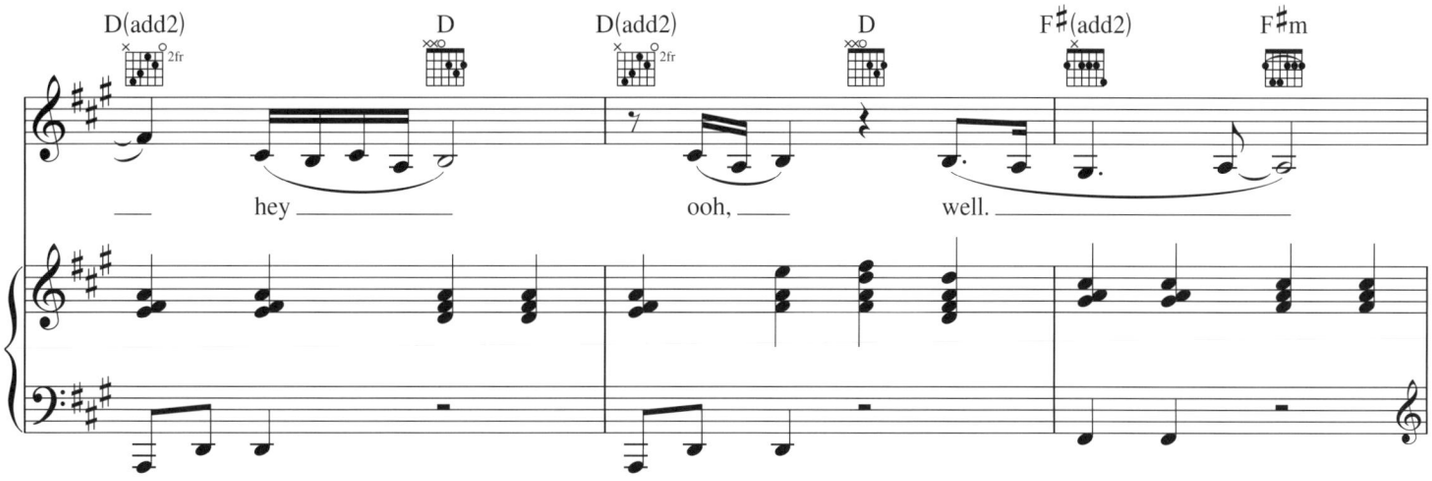
D(add2)
D
D(add2)
D
F♯(add2)
F♯m
hey
ooh,
well.

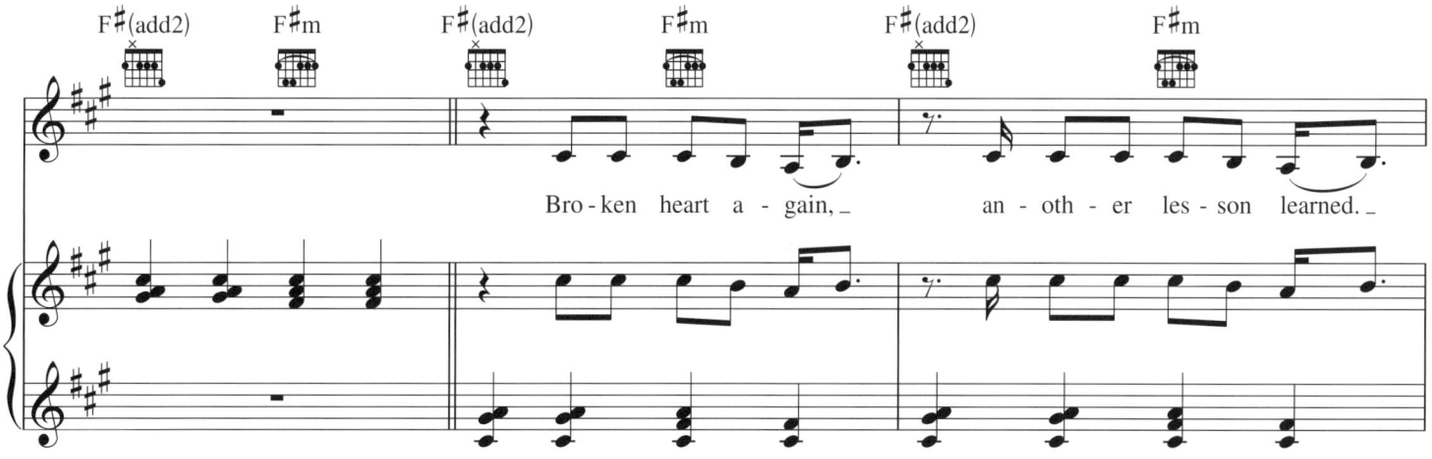
F♯(add2)
F♯m
F♯(add2)
F♯m
F♯(add2)
F♯m
Bro - ken heart a - gain,
an - oth - er les - son learned.

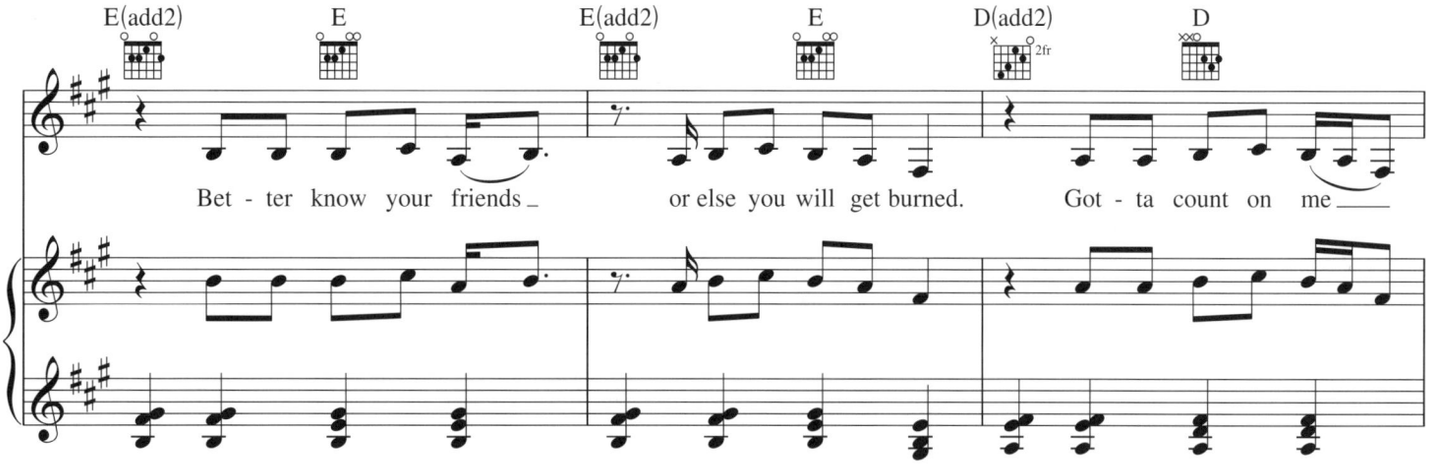
E(add2)
E
E(add2)
E
D(add2)
D
Bet - ter know your friends
or else you will get burned.
Got - ta count on me

D(add2)
2fr
D
F♯(add2)
F♯m
F♯(add2)
F♯m
'cause I can guar - an - tee that - a I'll be fine. No more
F♯(add2)
F♯m
F♯(add2)
F♯m
E(add2)
E
pain. No more pain. No more pain. No more
E(add2)
E
D(add2)
2fr
D
pain. No dra - ma,
(No more dra - ma in my life.
D(add9)
2fr
D
F♯(add2)
F♯m
no more in my life.
3
No one's gon - na make me hurt a - gain,

F♯(add2)
F♯m
F♯(add2)
F♯m
ooh.)
Why'd I play the fool,
F♯(add2)
F♯m
E(add2)
E
E(add2)
E
go through ups and downs, know-ing all the time you would-n't be a - round?
D(add2)
2fr
D
D(add2)
2fr
D
F♯(add2)
F♯m
But may-be I like the stress, 'cause I was young and rest-less. But that was long a - go.
F♯(add2)
N.C.
F♯(add2)
F♯m
F♯(add2)
F♯m
No more
I don't wan - na cry no more.
pain.
tears.
No more
No more

E(add2)
E
E(add2)
E
D(add2)
D
game.
fears.
No dra - ma,
D(add2)
D
F♯(add2)
F♯m
1
F♯(add2)
F♯m
no more in my life.
No more
2
F♯(add2)
F♯m
E/G♯
Gon-na speak my mind, o - kay.
Ooh, it feels so good when you
Dmaj7
E/G♯
G♯m7
C♯7
let go of all the dra - ma in your life.
Now you're free

Dmaj7
F♯m
from all the pain.
Free from all the game.
Free

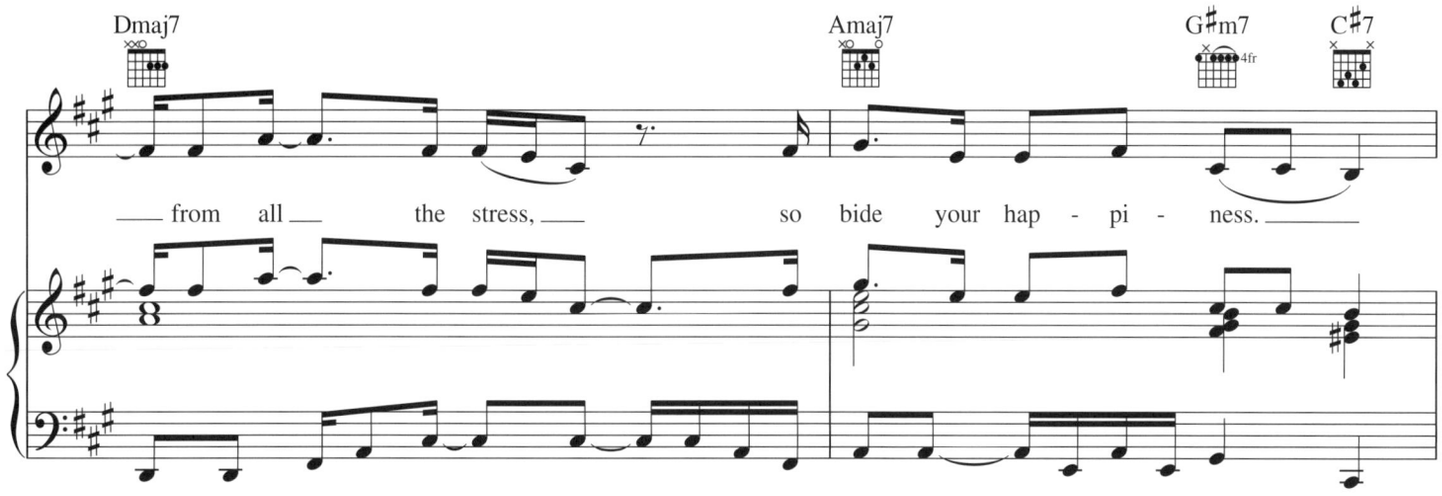
Dmaj7
Amaj7
G♯m7
4fr
C♯7
from all the stress,
so bide your hap - pi - ness.

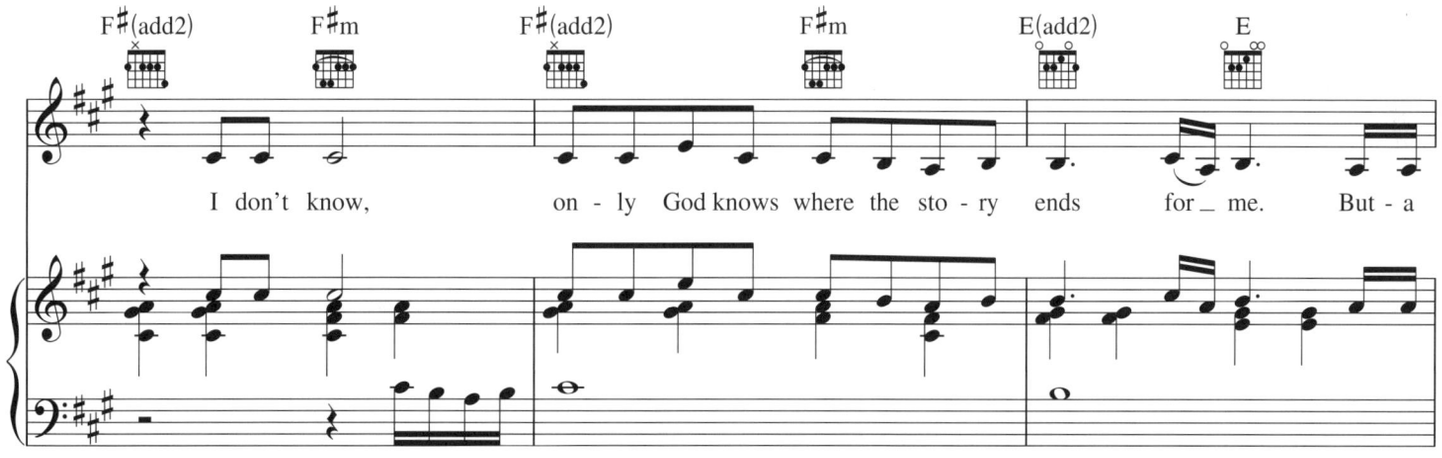
F♯(add2)
F♯m
F♯(add2)
F♯m
E(add2)
E
I don't know,
on - ly God knows where the sto - ry ends for me.
But - a

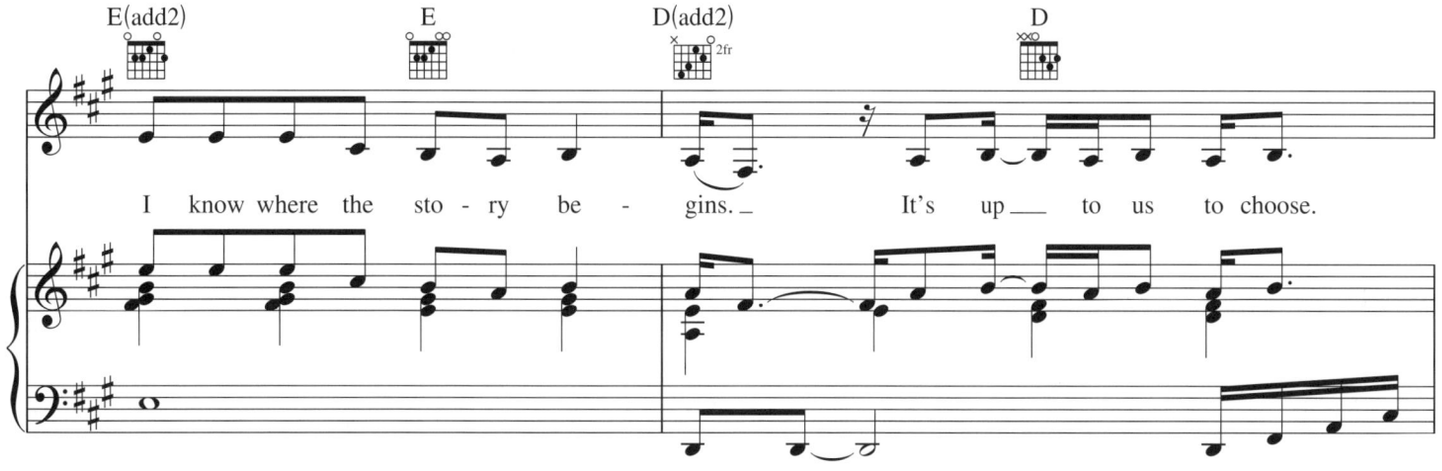
E(add2)
E
D(add2)
2fr
D
I know where the sto - ry be - gins.
It's up to us to choose.

D(add2)
2fr
D
F♯(add2)
F♯m
Wheth-er we win or lose.
And I choose to win,
F♯(add2)
N.C.
F♯(add2)
F♯m
F♯(add2)
F♯m
ooh.
No more
(1.,3.) pain.
(2.) tears.
No more
No more
E(add2)
E
E(add2)
E
D(add2)
2fr
D
game.
fears.
No dra - ma,
D(add2)
2fr
D
F♯(add2)
F♯m
1, 2
F♯(add2)
F♯m
no more in my life.
No more

3
F♯m(add2)
F♯m
E/G♯
A
C♯7
No more. No more dra - ma.
F♯m
E/G♯
A
C♯7
C♯7♯9
F♯m
E/G♯
No more dra - ma. No more
A
C♯7
C♯7♯9
F♯m
E/G♯
Dmaj7
F♯m
E/G♯
dra - ma. No more dra - ma. No more
A
C♯7
F♯m
E/G♯
A
C♯7
C♯7♯9
F♯m
E/G♯
dra - ma. No more dra - ma. No more

A
C♯7
C♯7♯9
F♯m
E/G♯
Dmaj7
F♯m
E/G♯
dra - ma.
No more
dra - ma.
No more
3
A
C♯7
F♯m
E/G♯
A
C♯7
dra - ma.
No more
dra - ma.
F♯m
E/G♯
Dmaj7
C♯m7
4fr
Bm7
A(add9)
Oh ___ no.
Oh no,
no more,
no more,
no more dra - ma.
No
G♯m7
4fr
C♯7sus
4fr
F♯m(add2)
F♯m
F♯m(add2)
F♯m
more dra - ma ___
in my, in my
life. ___
(Spoken:) I'm so tired.

E(add2)
E
E(add2)
E
D(add2)
2fr
D
I'm so tired, so tired.
So tired of all this drama.
Go a-head,

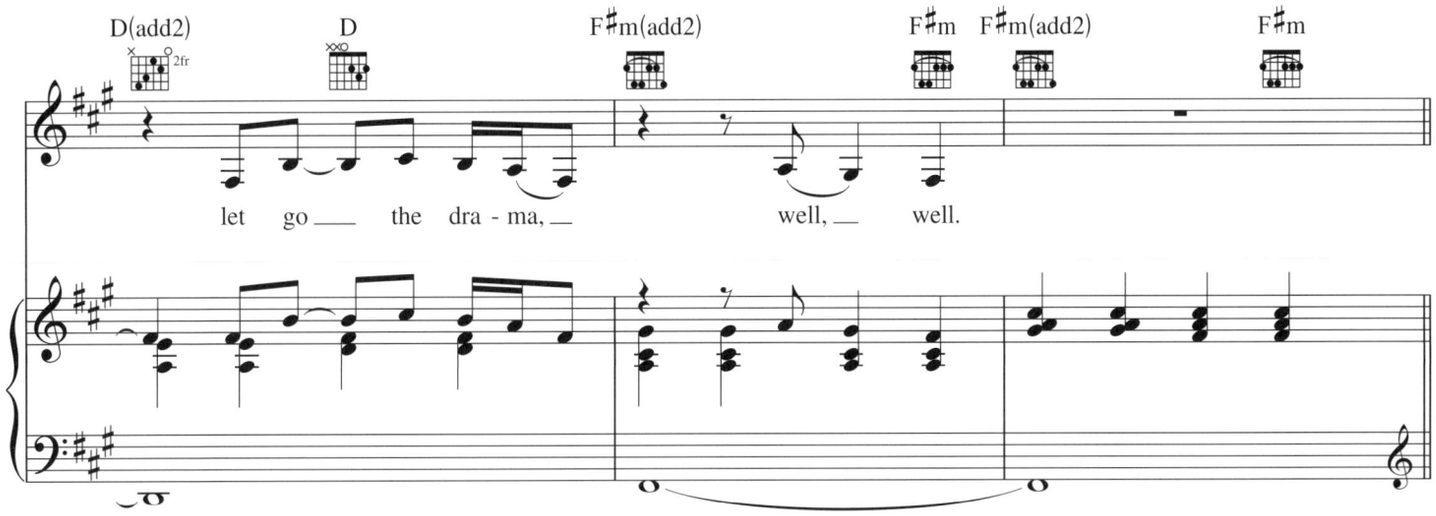
D(add2)
2fr
D
F♯m(add2)
F♯m
F♯m(add2)
F♯m
let go the dra-ma,
well, well.

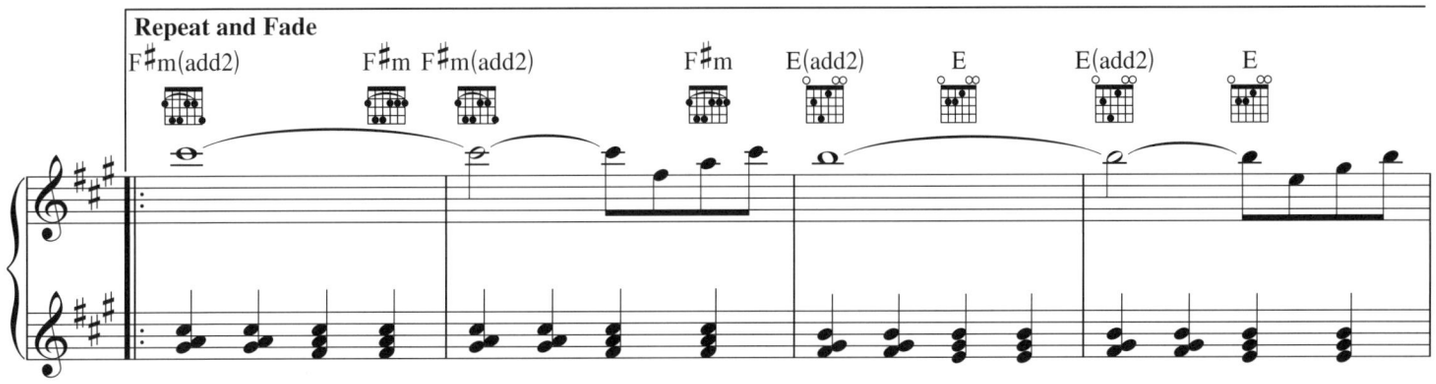
Repeat and Fade
F♯m(add2)
F♯m
F♯m(add2)
F♯m
E(add2)
E
E(add2)
E

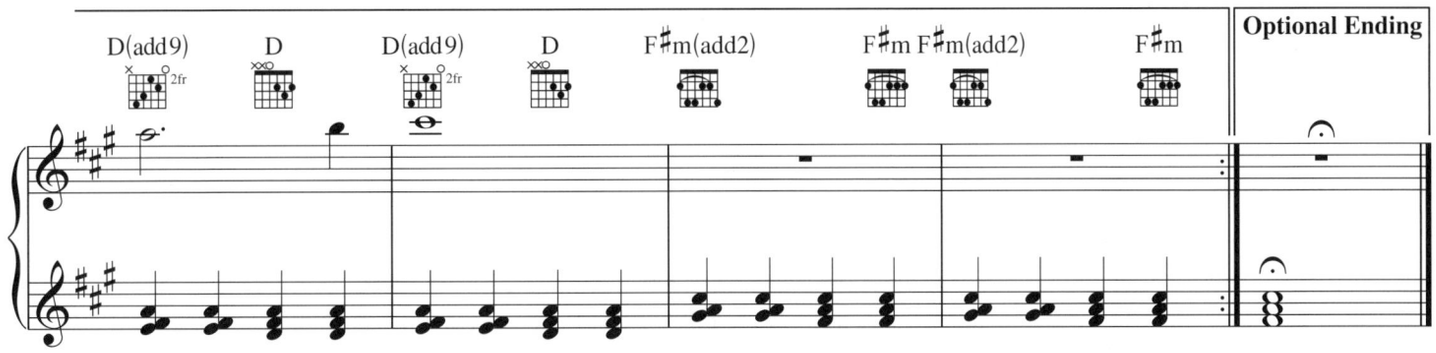
D(add9)
2fr
D
D(add9)
2fr
D
F♯m(add2)
F♯m
F♯m(add2)
F♯m
Optional Ending

FAMILY AFFAIR

Words and Music by ANDRE YOUNG,
MELVIN BRADFORD, MICHAEL ELIZONDO,
MARY J. BLIGE, CAMARA KAMBON, LUCHANA LODGE,
ASIA LOUIS and BRUCE MILLER

* *Recorded a half step higher.*

© AIN'T NOTHING BUT FUNKIN' MUSIC, MELVIN BRADFORD PUBLISHING DESIGNEE, HARD WORKING BLACK FOLKS INC., UNIVERSAL MUSIC CORP.,
MARY J. BLIGE MUSIC, UNIVERSAL TUNES, a division of SONGS OF UNIVERSAL, INC., CWAB, MUSIC OF WINDSWEPT, ELVIS MAMBO MUSIC,
FIVE CARD MUSIC, BLOTTER MUSIC, COLORSCAPES PUBLISHING, LUCHI PUBLISHING CO. and ASIAHTOWN ENTERTAINMENT
All Rights for MARY J. BLIGE MUSIC Controlled and Administered by UNIVERSAL MUSIC CORP.
All Rights for CWAB Controlled and Administered by UNIVERSAL TUNES, a division of SONGS OF UNIVERSAL, INC.
All Rights for ELVIS MAMBO MUSIC and FIVE CARD MUSIC Controlled and Administered by MUSIC OF WINDSWEPT
All Rights Reserved Used by Permission

Cm
3fr
me). Don't need no hate - a - ra - tion, hol - ler - a - tion (in this dance - a -
Gm
3fr
rie). Let's get it per - co - lat - ing while you're wait - ing (so just dance for
Cm
3fr
me).
Come on, ev - 'ry - bod - y, get on up, 'cause you know we gots to get it crunk.
Gm
3fr
Mar - y J. is in the spot to-night and I'm - 'a make you feel all right.
(Make you feel all right.)

Cm
3fr
Come on, ba - by, just par - ty with me.
Let loose and set your bod - y free.
Gm
3fr
Leave your sit - u - a - tions at the door so when you step in - side, jump on the floor.
Cm
3fr
Let's get it crunk; we're gon' have fun up on it (in this dance - a -
Gm
3fr
rie). We got y'all o - pen; now ya float - in' so you (gots to dance for

Cm
3fr
me). Don't need no hate - a - ra - tion, hol - ler - a - tion (in this dance - a -
Gm
3fr
1
rie). Let's get it per - co - lat - ing while you're wait - ing, (so just dance for
Ooh, ___ it's
Cm
3fr
me.)
on - ly gon - na be a - bout a mat - ter of time _ be - fore you get loose and start to lose your mind.
Gm
3fr
Cop you a drink; go 'head and rock your ice, 'cause we're cel - e - brat - ing no more dra - ma in our life. With a

Cm
3fr
great track pump - in', ev-'ry-bod-y's jump - in'. Go a - head and twist your back and get your bod-y bump - in'. I
Gm
3fr
told you, leave your sit - u - a-tions at the door, so grab some-bod-y and get your ass on the dance floor.
2
Cm11
while you're wait - ing, (so just dance for me.)
(So just dance, for we don't need no hat -
Gm11
ers; we're just try - ing to love one an - oth -

Cm
3fr
er. We just want y'all to have a good time. No more
Gm
3fr
dra - ma in your life. Work real hard to make a dime. If you got
Cm
3fr
beef, your prob - 'm not mine. Leave all that b. s. out - side; we're gon - na
Gm
3fr
cel - e - brate all night. Let's have fun to - night, no fights. Turn that

Cm
3fr
great track way up high. Mak - in' you dance all night, and I got some
Gm
3fr
real heat for you this time. It does - n't mat - ter if you're white or black; let's get
Cm
3fr
crunk, 'cause Mar - y's back.
Let's
me.) Let's
get it crunk; we're gon' have
Gm
3fr
fun up on it (in this dance - a - rie). We got y'all o - pen; now ya

Cm
3fr
float - 'in so you (gots to dance for me). Don't need no hate - a - ra - tion,
Gm
3fr
hol - ler - a - tion (in this dance - a - rie). Let's get it per - co - lat - ing
Repeat ad lib. and Fade
Optional Ending
Cm
3fr
while you're wait - ing, (so just dance for me.)
Gm
3fr

REAL LOVE

Words and Music by MARK C. ROONEY,
MARK MORALES and KIRK ROBINSON

Copyright © 1992 SONGS OF UNIVERSAL, INC., SECOND GENERATION ROONEY TUNES PUBLISHING, FIRST PRIORITY MUSIC PUBLISHING and HOT BUTTER MILK MUSIC, INC.
All Rights for SECOND GENERATION ROONEY TUNES PUBLISHING and FIRST PRIORITY MUSIC PUBLISHING Controlled and Administered by SONGS OF UNIVERSAL, INC.
All Rights Reserved Used by Permission

Dm7
Em7
Am7
you to re - al - ize I real - ly want to put you on. I've been search -
me how you fell for me, you said I'm not the one. So, I slow -
me in, to guide me towards a love my heart can feel. Now, I know
Dm7
Em7
Am7
- in' for some - one to sat - is - fy my ev - 'ry need. Won't you be
- ly came to see all of the things that you were made of, and now I hold
I can be faith - ful. I can be your all and all. I'll give you good lov -
Dm7
Em7
Am7
my in - spi - ra - tion, be the real love that I need? Yeah.
my dreams and in - spi - ra - tion, lead me to want some real,
- in' through the sum - mer - time, win - ter, spring and fall.
Dm7
Em7
Am7
Dm7
Em7
Real love,
real love.
Real love,
I'm search - ing for a real love, some -

Am7
Dm7
Em7
Am7
To Coda
- one to set my heart free. Real love, I'm search - ing for a
1
Dm7
Em7
Am7
real love. Ooh, when I met real love.
2
Dm7
Em7
I've
Am7
Dm7
got to have a real love, love so true
B7♯9
E7♯9
6fr
Am7
and oh, ba - by, I thought

Dm7
that love was you. I thought you were the an - swer to the ques-
B7♯9
E7♯9
6fr
Dm7
- tion in my mind, but it seems that I was wrong, if I stand strong,
E7♯9
6fr
Dm7
Em7
Am7
may - be I'll find our real love.
(Vocal 1st time only)
Dm7
Em7
1
Am7
2
Am7
D.S. al Coda
So, I've tried

CODA
Dm7
Em7
Am7
Dm7
Em7
real love.
Real love,
Am7
Dm7
Em7
Am7
I'm search - ing for a real love,
some - one to set my heart free.
Dm7
Em7
Am7
Dm7
Em7
Real love,
I'm
search - ing for
a
real love.
Am7
Play 4 times
N.C.
Real love.

NO ONE WILL DO

Words and Music by BUNNY SIGLER, ERICK ORTIZ,
KEVIN CROWE, CLIFFORD BROWN, III and DAVE YOUNG

* *Recorded a half step lower.*

© 2005 WARNER-TAMERLANE PUBLISHING CORP., WB MUSIC CORP., COLIONE CLIFF AND ROOK PUBLISHING, NOONTIME TUNES and HOTTER THAN U MUSIC
All Rights for NOONTIME TUNES and HOTTER THAN U MUSIC Administered by WARNER-TAMERLANE PUBLISHING CORP.
All Rights for COLIONE CLIFF AND ROOK PUBLISHING Administered by WB MUSIC CORP.
"No One Will Do" contains samples from "I Swear I Love No One But You" by Bunny Sigler © 1976 WARNER-TAMERLANE PUBLISHING CORP. (Renewed)
All Rights Reserved Used by Permission

C/F
3fr
Dm
C/F
3fr
Dm
I ain't got - ta knock on wood to tell y'all that I got it so good.
Am
C/G
C
C/G
C/F♯
He's ev - 'ry - thing that I need, and all that a man should be, and
C/F
3fr
Dm
C/F
3fr
Dm
put me on a flight if I wan - na; buy out the mall if I wan - na.
Am
C/G
C
C/G
C/F♯
(And I know y'all heard be - fore these same old met - a - phors, but my love is

C/F
3fr
Dm
C/F
3fr
Dm
so much more.) I don't wan - na change it; I don't wan - na do with - out you, ba -
Am
C/G
C
C/G
C/F♯
by.
('Cause he's just a - bove the rest; I must con - fess, the best love that I've
C/F
3fr
Dm
C/F
3fr
Dm
ev - er had.)
And I just got - ta let you know this:
(Don't let 'em
Am
C/G
C
C/G
C/F♯
tell you noth - in' dif - f'rent; you're the on - ly one I'm need - ing. I don't want

C/F
Dm
C/F
Dm
no one but you;
ba - by, no one will do.
And what they
Am
C/G
C
C/G
C/F♯
say don't e - ven mat - ter; they don't know what I know a - bout you.
I don't want
C/F
Dm
To Coda
C/F
Dm
no one but you.
Ba - by, no one will do.)
Am
C/G
C
C/G
C/F♯
It's me and him through the wi - re,
'cause when it comes to love, he de - liv - ers;

C/F
Dm
C/F
Dm
my per - son - al U - P - S.
I'm send - ing him an S - O - S that I
Am
C/G
C
Dm/G
C/F♯
(love him, and I want him, and I don't wan - na re - place him) with no - bod - y
C/F
Dm
C/F
Dm
else. I'm - a keep hold - in' on;
I'm - a keep the lov - in' strong.
Hey,
yeah.
Am
D.S. al Coda
(And I know y'all heard be - fore these
CODA
C/F
Dm
no one will do.)

Am
C/G
N.C.
Lead vocal ad lib.

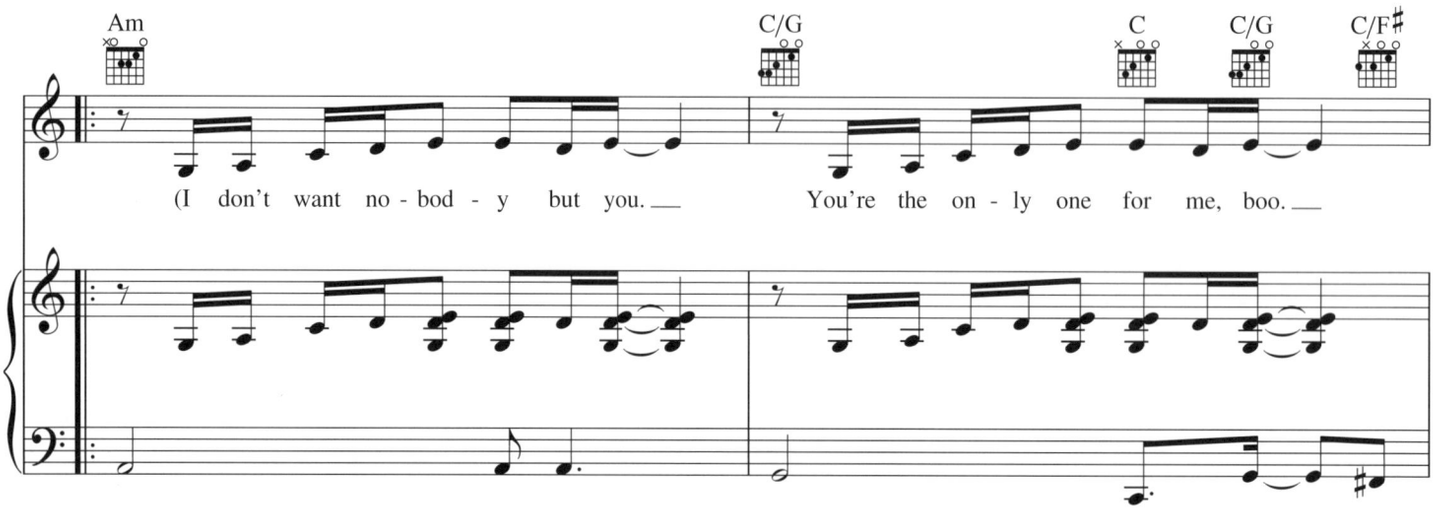
Am
C/G
C
C/G
C/F♯
(I don't want no - bod - y but you.
You're the on - ly one for me, boo.

C/F
3fr
Dm
Don't you know that you are the true.
1
C/F
3fr
Dm
I don't want no - bod - y but you.)

2
C/F
3fr
Dm
Am
I don't want no-bod - y but you.)
(1.) (Don't let 'em tell you noth - in' dif - f'rent; you're the on - ly
(2.,3.) Lead vocal ad lib.

C/G
C
C/G
C/F♯
C/F
3fr
Dm
one I'm need - ing. I don't want no one but you; ba - by,
C/F
3fr
Dm
Am
no one will do. And what they say don't e - ven mat - ter; they don't know what I
C/G
C
C/G
C/F♯
C/F
3fr
Dm
1, 2
C/F
3fr
Dm
know a - bout you. I don't want no one but you. Ba - by, no one will do.)
3
F
Dm7
Am
8va
rit.

BE WITHOUT YOU

Words and Music by MARY J. BLIGE,
JOHNTA AUSTIN, BRYAN MICHAEL COX
and JASON PERRY

Copyright © 2005 UNIVERSAL MUSIC CORP., MARY J. BLIGE MUSIC, CHRYSALIS MUSIC, NAKED UNDER MY CLOTHES, W.B.M. MUSIC CORP.,
NOONTIME SOUTH, INC., BABYBOY'S LITTLE PUBLISHING COMPANY and JASON'S LYRICS
All Rights for MARY J. BLIGE MUSIC Controlled and Administered by UNIVERSAL MUSIC CORP.
All Rights for NAKED UNDER MY CLOTHES Controlled and Administered by CHRYSALIS MUSIC
All Rights Reserved Used by Permission

C
Am7
Dm
Gm9
3fr
oh, oh, ooh.
C
A7
N.C.
Chem-is-try was cra-zy from the get go. Nei-ther one of us knew why.
We did-n't deal noth-in' o-ver-night 'cause a love like this takes some time.
Dm
B♭maj7
Peo-ple swore it off as a phase, said we can't see that. Now

C
Am7
Dm
Gm9
3fr
from top to bot-tom they see that we did that. Yes, it's so true that, yes, we been through it.
C
A7
Dm
B♭maj7
Yes, but we got real shit. Yes, see ba-by, we been too strong for too long and I can't be with-out
C
Am7
Dm
Gm9
3fr
you, ba - by. And I'll be wait-in' up un-til you get home 'cause I can't sleep with-out
C
A7
Dm
B♭maj7
you, ba - by. An-y-bod-y who's ev-er loved ya know just what I feel.

C
Am7
Dm
Gm9
3fr
Too hard to fake it. Noth-in' can re-place it. Call the ra-di-o if you just can't be with-out your ba-by.
C
A7
To Coda I
To Coda II
Dm
B♭maj7
I got a ques-tion for ya, see I al-read-y know the
C
Am7
Dm
Gm9
3fr
an-swer. Still I wan-na ask you, would you lie? No. Make me cry? No. Do some-
C
A7
Dm
B♭maj7
thin' be-hind my back and then try cov-er it up? Well, nei-ther would I, ba-

C
Am7
Dm
Gm9
3fr
- by. My love is on - ly ev-'ry love. Yes, I'll be faith - ful. Yes, love for real.

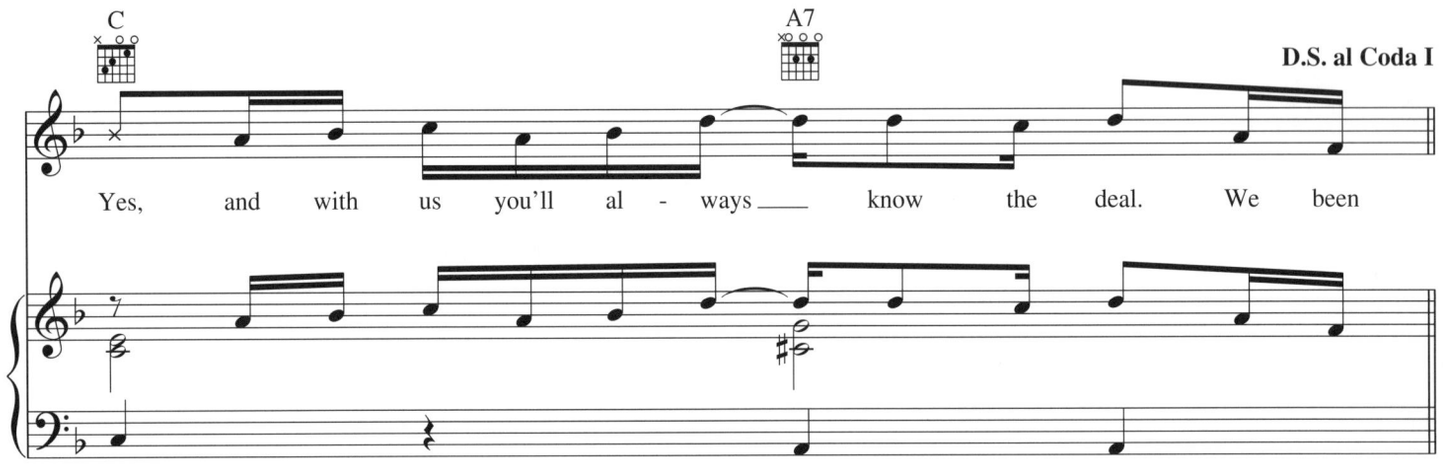
C
A7
D.S. al Coda I
Yes, and with us you'll al - ways know the deal. We been

CODA I
Gm7
Am7
B♭maj7
Am7
See this is real talk, I'm 'a al-ways stay no mat - ter what. Through the

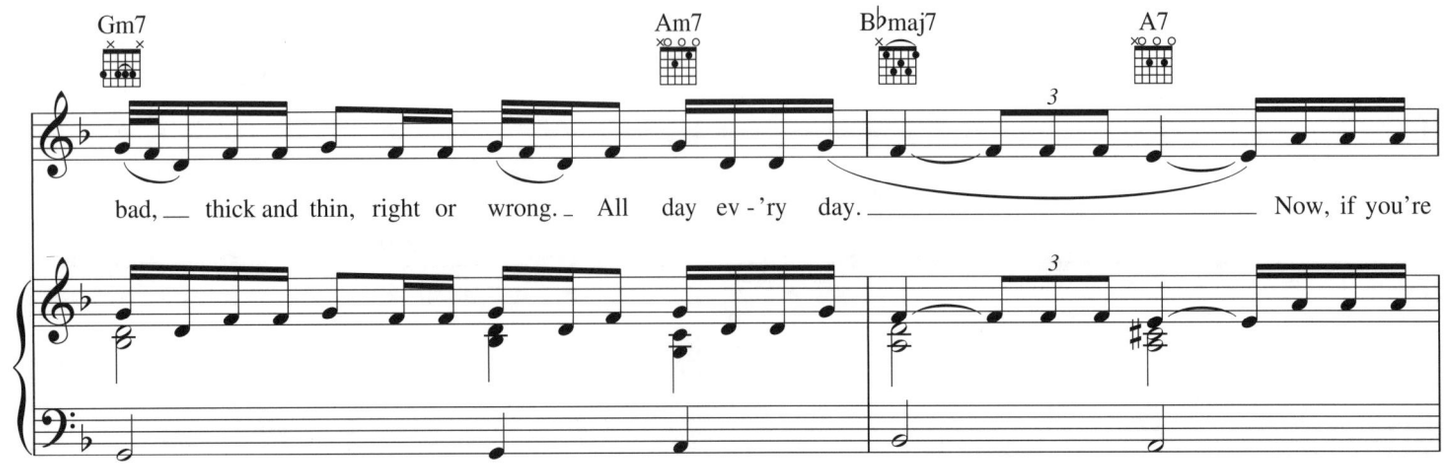
Gm7
Am7
B♭maj7
A7
bad, thick and thin, right or wrong. All day ev - 'ry day. Now, if you're

Dm
N.C.
down on love or don't be - lieve this ain't for you. No, this ain't for you.
And if you got it
deep in your heart, and deep down you know that it's true, well, let me see ya' put your
Come on, come on, come on.
Dm
B♭maj7
C
Am7
hands up, hands up. Fel - las, tell your la - dy she's the one. Oh, put your
Dm
Gm9
3fr
C
A7
D.S.S. al Coda II
hands up, hands up. La-dies, let him know he's got your love.
Look him right in his eyes and tell him. We been

CODA II
Dm
B♭maj7
C
Am7
Dm
Gm9
3fr
C
A7
Dm
B♭maj7
I wan-na be with you, got-ta be with you, need to be with you.
C
Am7
Dm
Gm9
3fr
I wan-na be with you, got-ta be with you, need to be with you.
C
A7
Repeat and Fade
Optional Ending
Dm

I'M GOING DOWN

Words and Music by
NORMAN WHITFIELD

Copyright © 1976 USI B MUSIC PUBLISHING
Copyright Renewed
All Rights Controlled and Administered by SONGS OF UNIVERSAL, INC.
All Rights Reserved Used by Permission

Am7
G
a - gainst my win-dow-pane is slow - ly, is slow - ly driv-ing me in -
Look what you done to me. I can't stop these tears from fall - ing from my
Am7
N.C.
G6
sane. Boy,
eyes. Ba - by,
I'm go - ing down. I'm go - ing
F6
G6
down 'cause you ain't a - round. Ba - by, my
1
Am
Bm
C
N.C.
whole world's up - side
2,3
Am
Bm
C
N.C.
whole world's up - side

G
Am7
down.
Ooh, ba - by love.
G
Am7
To Coda
Go - ing down, go - ing down.
G
Am7
G
Go-ing down.
Ooh,
Am7
D.S. al Coda
(take 2nd ending)
I, I, I'm go-ing
CODA
G
Oh, I don't know what to do
I do wrong? I said,

Am7
G
if I ev - er lose you.
I'll be go - ing down.
what did I do wrong?
Please, for - give me, ba - by,
Am7
G
I said I'll be go - ing down.
and come on home.
Go - ing down,
Am7
G
Please, for - give me, ba - by.
I'm so sor - ry, sor - ry, sor - ry,
go - ing down,
go - ing down.
1
Am7
2
Am7
G
sor - ry.
What did
rit.

911

Words and Music by WYCLEF JEAN,
JERRY DUPLESSIS, MARY BROWN
and KATIA CADET

Moderately slow

Em Bm7 Am7

(Spoken:) Yo, what up? This Wyclef with Mary J. I like to serenade the girls with

p

G Bm Em Bm7

my acoustic guitar. You know what I'm sayin'? Yo, fellas havin' problems with your chicks, I want you right now to turn the lights

Am7 G Bm Em

down low. Pull your girl up next to you. I want you to say these words to her.

If death comes for me to - night,_ girl,

Copyright © 2000 Sony/ATV Music Publishing LLC, Huss-Zwingli Publishing Inc., EMI Blackwood Music Inc.,
Te-Bass Music Inc., Miss Mary's Music and Baby Kat's Music
All Rights on behalf of Sony/ATV Music Publishing LLC and Huss-Zwingli Publishing Inc. Administered by
Sony/ATV Music Publishing LLC, 8 Music Square West, Nashville, TN 37203
All Rights on behalf of Te-Bass Music Inc. Controlled and Administered by EMI Blackwood Music Inc.
International Copyright Secured All Rights Reserved

Bm7
2 fr
Am7
G
Bm
I want you to know that I loved you.
And no
Em
Bm7
2 fr
Am7
mat-ter how tough I would-'ve dared,
on-ly to you I would re-veal my tears.
G
Bm
Em
Bm7
2 fr
See, tell the po-lice I ain't home to-night.
Mess-in' a-round with you is gon-na
Am7
G
Bm
Em
get me life.
But when I look in-to your eyes,

Bm7
2 fr
Am7
G
Bm
man, you're worth that sac - ri - fice, yeah, yeah. If
Em
Bm7
2 fr
Am7
this is the kind of love that my mom used to warn me a - bout, man, I'm in trou - ble. I'm in real big
this is the kind of love that your mom used to warn you a - bout, Mar - y, you're in trou - ble. You're in real big
G
Bm
Em
Bm7
2 fr
trou - ble.
trou - ble.
If this is the kind of love that the old folks used to warn me a-bout, man, I'm in
Am7
G
Bm
Em
trou - ble. I'm in real big trou - ble. Some-one please call 9 - 1 -
(1.) (Spoken:) I need y'all to do me a favor.
(2.) (Spoken:) You got anything to say, girl?

Bm7
2 fr
Am7
G
Bm
1. Pick up the phone, yo. Tell them I've just been shot down and the bul-let's in my
Tell them I've just got shot down, tell them I just got shot
Em
Bm
Am7
heart. And it's pierc - ing through my soul. I'm los-in' blood, yo. Feel my bod - y get - tin'
down.
G
Bm7
2 fr
Em
Bm7
2 fr
cold. Some-one please call 9 - 1 - 1. Pick up the
Can you do that
Am7
G
Bm
Em
phone, yo. The al - leg - ed as - sail - ant is five - foot - one and she shot me through my
for me? The al - leg - ed as - sail - ant was five - foot - one and she shot me through my

Bm7
2 fr
Am7
To Coda
soul.
soul.
Feel my bod - y get - tin' cold,
G
Bm
Em
so cold.
Some-times I feel like I'm a pris - on - er.
Bm7
2 fr
Am7
I think I'm trapped here for a while.
But I'm
G
Bm
Em
al-ways right here with you, girl.
And ev - 'ry breath I fight to take,
3
3

Bm7
2 fr
Am7
yeah, it's as hard as these four walls I wan - na break.
G
Bm
Em
Mm, I told the cops you was-n't here to-night.
Bm7
2 fr
Am7
Mess-in' a - round with me is gon - na get you life,
G
Bm
Em
oh yeah, yeah. But ev - 'ry time I look in - to your eyes,

Bm7
2 fr
Am7
G
Bm
D.S. al Coda
then it's worth the sac - ri - fice,
yeah, yeah. If
CODA
G
Bm
Em
Bm7
2 fr
Wy - clef and Mar-y J. Blige. I'm feel-in' you, girl,
Am7
G
Bm
Repeat and Fade
Em
I un-der-stand.
(Lead vocal ad lib)
Bm7
2 fr
Am7
G
Bm
Optional Ending
Em

NOT GON' CRY

from the Original Soundtrack Album WAITING TO EXHALE

Words and Music by
BABYFACE

Copyright © 1995 Sony/ATV Songs LLC, ECAF Music and Fox Film Music Corp.
All Rights on behalf of Sony/ATV Music Publishing LLC and ECAF Music Administered by Sony/ATV Music Publishing LLC, 8 Music Square West, Nashville, TN 37203
International Copyright Secured All Rights Reserved

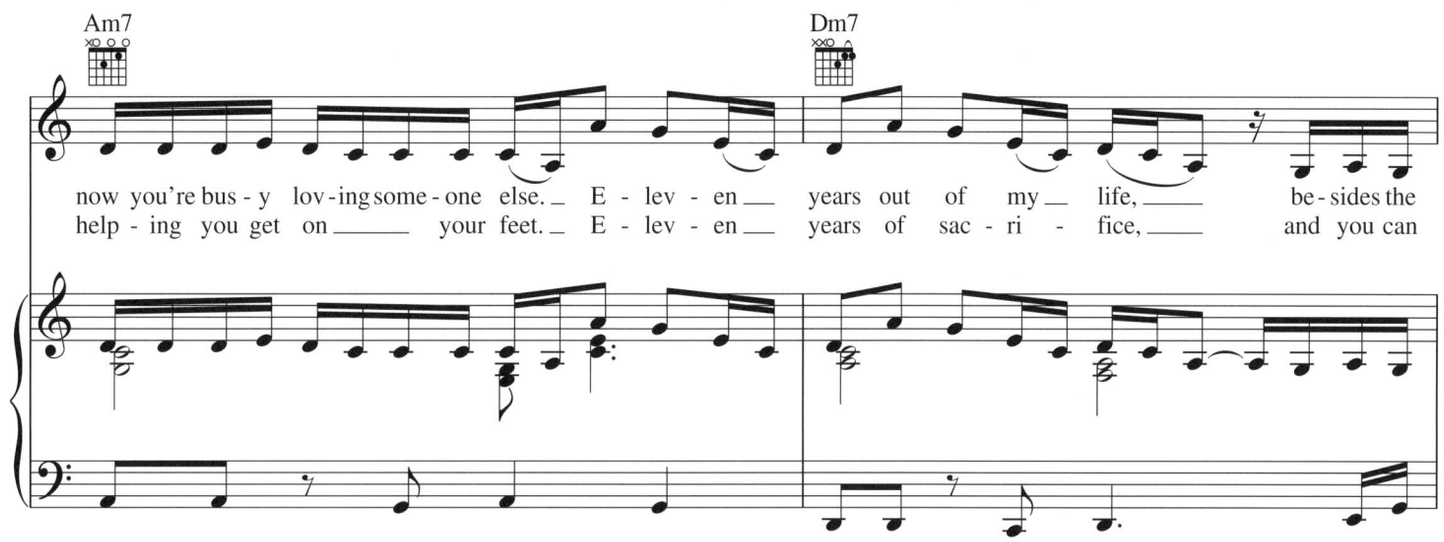
Am7
Dm7
now you're bus - y lov - ing some - one else. E - lev - en years out of my life, be - sides the
help - ing you get on your feet. E - lev - en years of sac - ri - fice, and you can

Am7
Dm7
kids, I have noth - ing to show. Wast - ed my years, a fool of a wife. I should - a
leave me at the drop of a dime. Swal - lowed my fears, stood by your side. I should - a

To Coda
Fmaj7/G
Fmaj7
Csus2/E
Am7
left your ass long time a - go.
left your ass a thou - sand times.
Well, I'm not gon' cry, I'm not gon' cry. I'm

Dm7
F/G
Dm7
Em7
Fmaj7
Csus2/E
Am7
not gon' shed no tears. No, I'm not gon' cry, it's not the time ___ 'cause
you're not worth _ my tears. Well, I'm not gon' cry, I'm not gon' cry. I'm
not gon' shed no tears. No, I'm not gon' cry, it's not the time ___ 'cause
1
Dm7/G
F/G
you're not worth _ my tears.
2
Dm7/G
F/G
you're not worth _ my tears.

C
C7/B♭
5fr
I know there are no guar - an - tees,
in love
you take your chanc - es.
But
F/A
Fm/A♭
some-how it seems un - fair
to me, so
un - fair, look at the cir - cum - stanc - es.
Through
C/G
Am11
3fr
sick - ness and health, 'til death do us part,
those were the words that we said from our heart.
So
B♭
Fmaj7/G
D.S. al Coda
(take 2nd verse)
now when you say
that you're leav-ing me,
I don't
get that part,
oh.

CODA
Fmaj7
Csus2/E
Am7
Dm7
F/G
Dm7
Em7
not gon' cry, I'm not gon' cry. I'm not gon' shed no tears. No, I'm
not gon' cry, it's not the time 'cause you're not worth my tears. Well, I'm
not gon' cry, I'm not gon' cry. I'm not gon' shed no tears. No, I'm
Repeat and Fade
Optional Ending
Cmaj9
Fmaj7/G
not gon' cry, it's not the time 'cause you're not worth my tears. Well, I'm not gon' cry.

MY LIFE '06

Words and Music by SEAN COMBS,
MARY J. BLIGE, CHUCKY THOMPSON,
ARLENE DELVALLE and ROY AYERS

© 1991, 1994 EMI APRIL MUSIC INC., JUSTIN COMBS PUBLISHING COMPANY INC., UNIVERSAL MUSIC CORP., MARY J. BLIGE MUSIC,
SONY/ATV MUSIC PUBLISHING LLC, NINTH STREET TUNNEL MUSIC INC., DOOCH MUSIC, CHRYSALIS MUSIC and AYERS ROY UBIQUITY INC.
All Rights for JUSTIN COMBS PUBLISHING COMPANY INC. Controlled and Administered by EMI APRIL MUSIC INC.
All Rights for MARY J. BLIGE MUSIC Controlled and Administered by UNIVERSAL MUSIC CORP.
All Rights for SONY/ATV MUSIC PUBLISHING LLC and NINTH STREET TUNNEL MUSIC INC. Administered by SONY/ATV MUSIC PUBLISHING LLC
8 Music Square West, Nashville, TN 37203
All Rights for AYERS ROY UBIQUITY INC. Administered by CHRYSALIS MUSIC
All Rights Reserved International Copyright Secured Used by Permission
-contains elements of "Everybody Loves The Sunshine" by Roy Ayers

E♭m7
A♭13
D♭maj9
C7♭9
Fm9
Cm9
A♭m13
(My life, my life, my life my life, in the sun - shine.) If you looked in my life and see what I've
B♭m9
Fm9
Cm9
A♭m13
seen, la, da, da, da, da, if you looked in my life and see what I've
B♭m9
Fm9
Cm9
A♭m13
seen, la, da, da, da, da, if you looked in my life and see what I've

B♭m9
6fr
Fm9
Cm9
A♭m13
3fr
seen, la, da, da, da, da, if you looked in my life and see what I've
𝄋
(My life, my life, my life, my life in the sun - shine.) Life can be on - ly what
seen. Take your time, ba - by, don't
you make it. When you're feel - ing down, you
you rush a thing. Don't you know I know we
should nev - er fake it. Say what's on your mind
all are strug - gling? I know it is hard,

B♭m9
6fr
Fm9
Cm9
A♭m13
3fr
and you'll find in time that all the neg - a - tive en -
but we will get by, and if you don't be - lieve
B♭m9
6fr
Fm9
Dm11
3fr
D♭maj7/E♭
6fr
er - gy, it will all de - cease
in me, just be - lieve in Him,
Fm9
Dm11
3fr
D♭maj7/E♭
6fr
and you'll be at peace with your - self.
'cause He'll give you peace of mind
Fm9
Dm11
3fr
D♭maj7/E♭
6fr
You won't real - ly need no one else
and you will see the sun shine

Fm9
Dm11
3fr
D♭maj7/E♭
6fr
ex - cept for the man a - bove,
and you'll get to free your mind

E♭m7
6fr
A♭13
4fr
D♭maj9
3fr
be - cause He'll give you love.
and things will turn out fine.

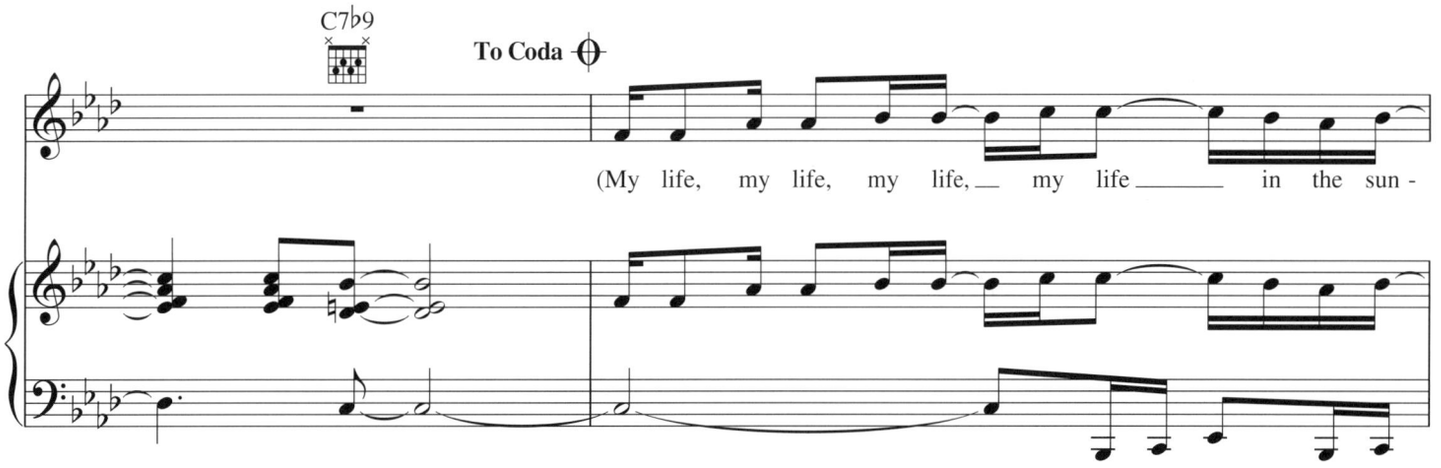
C7♭9
To Coda
(My life, my life, my life, my life in the sun -

Fm9
Cm9
A♭m13
3fr
B♭m9
6fr
- shine.) If you looked in my life and see what I've seen,

Fm9
Cm9
A♭m13
3fr
B♭m9
6fr
if you looked in my life and see what I've seen,
if you looked in my life and see what I've seen,
if you looked in my life and see what I've seen.
(My life, my life, my life, my life.)
D.S. al Coda
CODA
(My life, my life, my life, my life.)

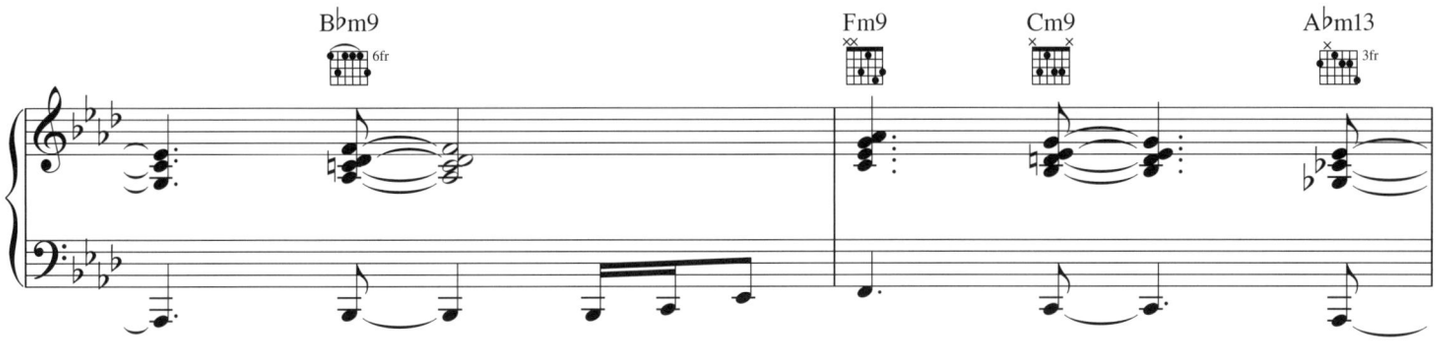
B♭m9
6fr
Fm9
Cm9
A♭m13
3fr

B♭m9
6fr
Fm9
Cm9
A♭m13
3fr
I got - ta go through the fi - re and raise the flame, let it

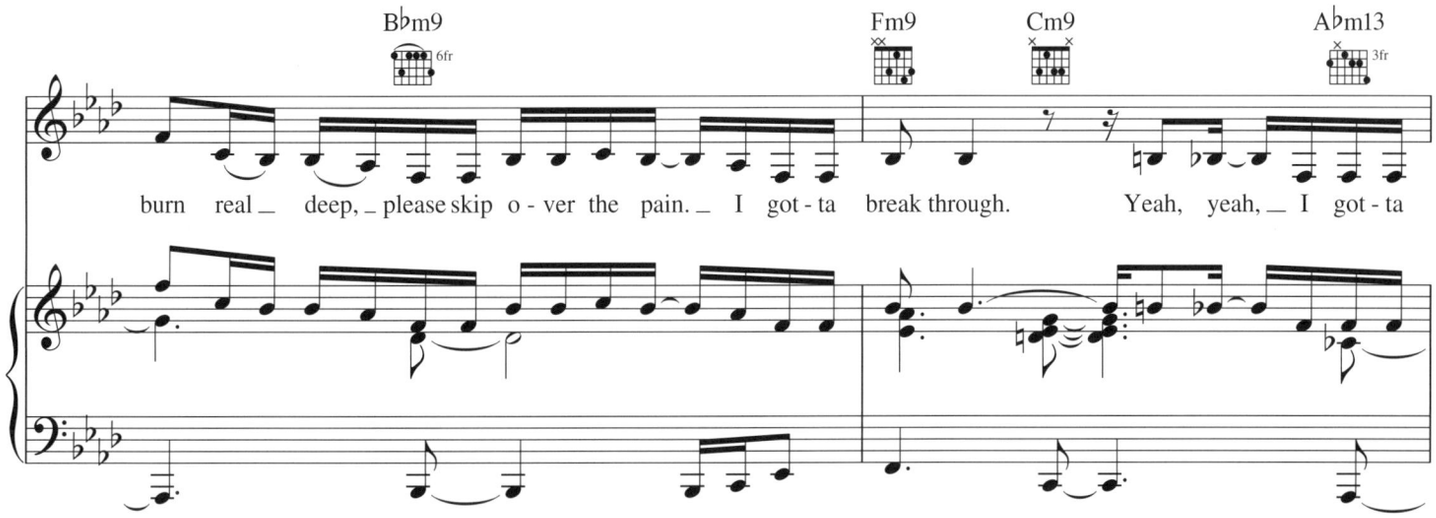
B♭m9
6fr
Fm9
Cm9
A♭m13
3fr
burn real deep, please skip o - ver the pain. I got - ta break through. Yeah, yeah, I got - ta

B♭m9
6fr
Fm9
Cm9
A♭m13
3fr
break through. I'm rec - og - niz - in' the man in the mir - ror was me that was

B♭m9
6fr
Fm9
Cm9
A♭m13
3fr
hurt - in' my - self in re - al - i - ty. I had to break through. Oh, I had to
B♭m9
6fr
Fm9
Cm9
A♭m13
3fr
break through. You know
B♭m9
6fr
Fm9
Cm9
A♭m13
3fr
what I'm talk - in' 'bout, yeah. I'm talk - in' 'bout get - tin' it to - geth - er,
B♭m9
6fr
Fm9
Cm9
A♭m13
3fr
yeah, uh. I'm talk - in' 'bout deal - in' with the pres - sure. I'm talk - in' 'bout

B♭m9
6fr
Fm9
Cm9
A♭m13
3fr
let - tin' it burn. Let it burn. Let it burn. Let it burn. Let it burn, yeah,
oh. If you looked in my life and see what I've
seen, if you looked in my life and see what I've
seen, if you looked in my life and see what I've

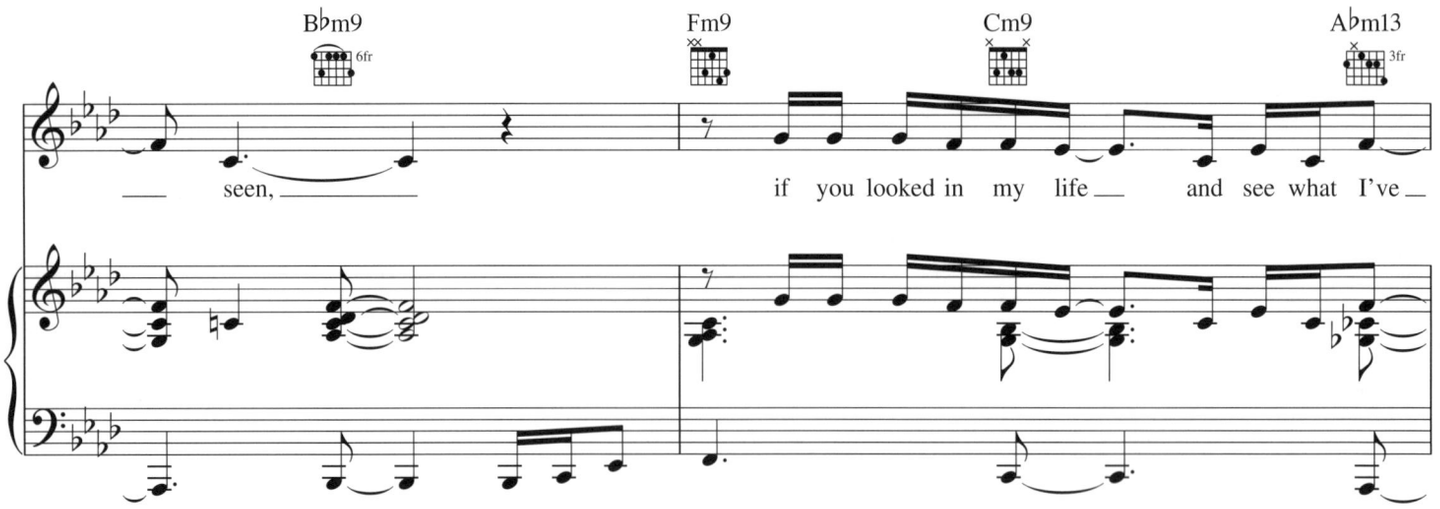
B♭m9
6fr
Fm9
Cm9
A♭m13
3fr
seen,
if you looked in my life
and see what I've

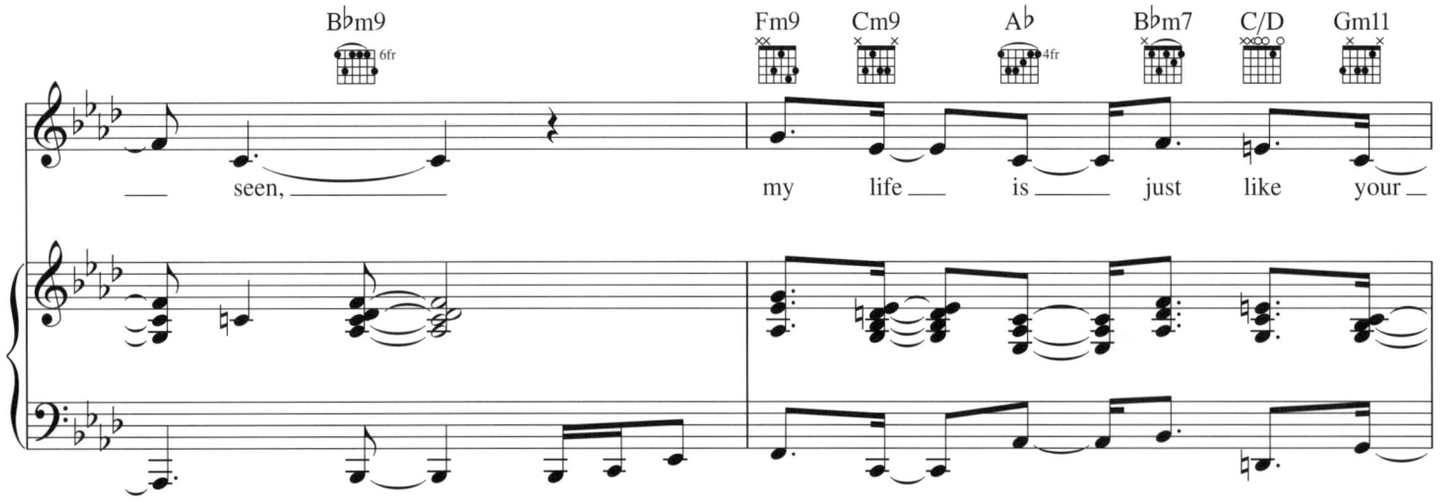
B♭m9
6fr
Fm9
Cm9
A♭
4fr
B♭m7
C/D
Gm11
seen,
my life
is
just like your

C7♯9(♭13)
2fr
Fm9
life,
oh.
rit.

BE HAPPY

Words and Music by SEAN COMBS,
MARY J. BLIGE, ARLENE DELVALLE, JEAN C. OLIVIER,
CURTIS MAYFIELD and GILBERT ASKEY

© 1994 EMI APRIL MUSIC INC., JUSTIN COMBS PUBLISHING, INC., UNIVERSAL MUSIC CORP.,
MARY J. BLIGE MUSIC, JELLY'S JAMS LLC, DOOCH MUSIC, JUMPING BEAN SONGS LLC,
TWELVE AND UNDER MUSIC, WARNER-TAMERLANE PUBLISHING CORP. and ANDRASK MUSIC
All Rights for JUSTIN COMBS PUBLISHING, INC. Controlled and Administered by EMI APRIL MUSIC INC.
All Rights for MARY J. BLIGE MUSIC Controlled and Administered by UNIVERSAL MUSIC CORP.
All Rights Reserved International Copyright Secured Used by Permission

love my - self e - nough to know when it's time,
time to let go?
Chorus
Sing, All I real - ly want is to be hap - py, to
find a love that's mine. It would be so sweet. All I real - ly want is to

be hap - py, to find a love that's mine. It would
To Coda
be so sweet. I guess you're a sign from the sweet Lord a - bove.
I know the an - swer is in front of me, but when
You think you're in love, you on - ly see what you wan - na see. And

all I see is me for you and you for me. Oh,
Fm9
I can - not hide the way I feel in - side.
I don't know why, but ev - 'ry day I wan - na cry. If I give
you one more try to these rules will you a - bide? And if I mean

an - y - thing to you, would it make ev - 'ry - thing all right?
Dm9
All I real - ly want is to be hap - py, to
find a love that's mine. It would be so sweet. All I real - ly want is to
be hap - py, to find a love that's mine. It would

Fm9
be so sweet. I just wan-na
be so, so hap - py, but the
an - swer lies in me. I do
be - lieve that we can be hap - py. I said I wan-na be hap -

Additional Lyrics

2. Life is too short to be trying to play some games.
Now take some time and you think about if it's really worth losin' me.
Why must it be this way? Why do you have to play with my mind all the time?
Help me sing it.

Chorus

I'LL BE THERE FOR YOU/ YOU'RE ALL I NEED TO GET BY

I'LL BE THERE FOR YOU
Words and Music by CLIFFORD SMITH
and ROBERT F. DIGGS JR.

YOU'RE ALL I NEED TO GET BY
Words and Music by NICKOLAS ASHFORD
and VALERIE SIMPSON

Moderate Hip-Hop

I'LL BE THERE FOR YOU
Copyright © 1995 by Universal Music - Careers, Wu-Tang Publishing and Ramecca Publishing
All Rights Administered by Universal Music - Careers
International Copyright Secured All Rights Reserved

YOU'RE ALL I NEED TO GET BY
© 1968 (Renewed 1994) JOBETE MUSIC CO., INC.
All Rights Controlled and Administered by EMI APRIL MUSIC INC.
All Rights Reserved International Copyright Secured Used by Permission

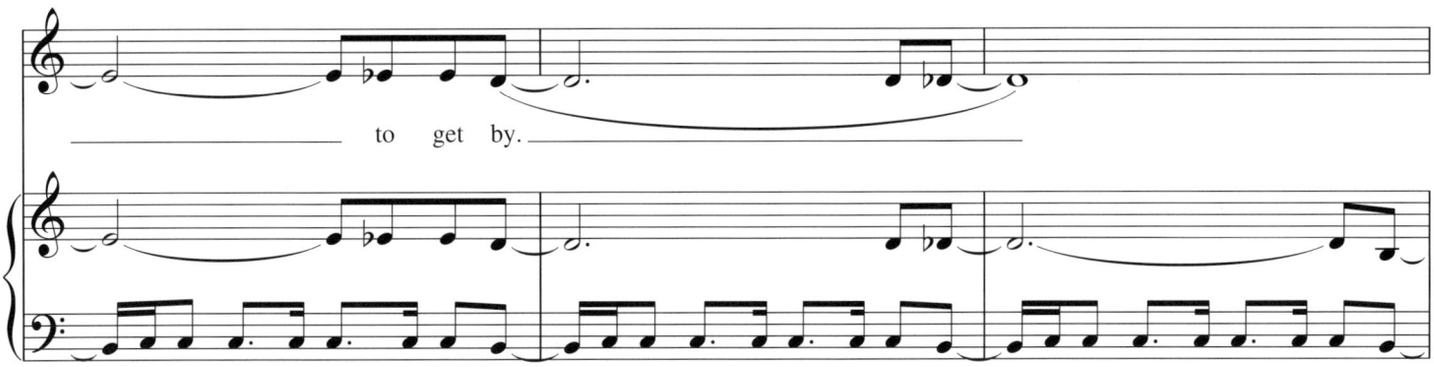
to get by.

Short - y, I'm there for you an - y - time you need me. For real, girl, it's me in your world, be - lieve me.

Noth - in' make a man feel bet - ter than a wom - an, queen wit' a crown that be down for what - ev - er.

There are few things that's for - ev - er, my la - dy, we can make war or make ba - bies. Back when I was

noth - in' you made a broth - er feel like he was some - thin'. That's why I'm wit' you 'til this day, boo, no front - in'.

E - ven when the skies were gray you would rub me on my back and say, "Ba - by, it - 'll be o - kay." Now that's

real to a broth - er like me, ba - by. Nev - er, ev - er give my boot - y a - way and keep it tight, all right?

And I'm - a walk these dogs so we can live in a phat - ass crib wit' thou - sands of kids. Word

life, you don't need a ring to be my wife. Just be there for me and I'm a make sure we be

liv - in' in the fuck - in' lap of lux - u - ry. I'm re - al - iz - in' that you did - n't have to fuck wit' me, but you

did. Now I'm go - in' all out, kid, and I got mad love to give. You my nig - ga.
You're all

I need to get by.

You're all
I need
to get by.

I got a love jonze for your bod-y and your skin tone.

Five min-utes a-lone, I'm al-read-y on the roam,
plus I love the fact you got a mind of your own. No

need to shop a-round, you got the good shit at home.
E-ven if I'm locked up north, you in the world wrapped in

three fourths of the cloth, nev - er show - in' your stuff _ off, boo. __ It be true, me for you, that's how it is.

I can be your No - ah, you can be my wiz, then I can be your sun, you can be my earth.

Res - ur - rect - in' God through birth, that's be - lief. You're all that I need, I'll be there for you. _ If you

keep it real wit' me, I'll keep it real wit' you. ___ Love in your whole steeze, it be in there, boo. _ On top of
You're all _____ I need ___

that, you got the good pow - er, you. You're all that I need, I'll be there for you. If you
to get by.
keep it real wit' me I'll keep it real wit' you. Love in your whole steeze, it be in there, boo. On top of
You're all I need
that, you got the good pow - er, you.
to get by.
You're all I need

to get by.
You're all I need to get by.
Repeat and Fade
Optional Ending
You're all I need
to get by.